THE
MODEST
MODEL™
FOR HEALING & DELIVERANCE

DR. LAVITA S. MODEST
FOREWORD BY DR. VEONTAE R. MANN

Published by So It Is Written, LLC
Rochester, MI
SoItIsWritten.net

The Modest Model™ for Healing & Deliverance
Copyright © 2025 by Dr. Lavita S. Modest

Edited by: So It Is Written – www.SoItIsWritten.net

Formatting: Ya Ya Ya Creative – YaYaYaCreative@gmail.com

ISBN: 979-8-9993606-0-1

LCCN: 2025913598

PRINTED AND BOUND IN THE UNITED STATES OF AMERICA

DEDICATION

First and foremost, I dedicate this work to my loving
Heavenly Father, God. To my big brother, Jesus Christ, and
to the co-author, Holy Spirit. Without them, this project
would not be possible. Additionally, I must salute my
husband, Eric, who is my biggest inspiration and source of
encouragement. To my miracle babies, Chelsi, and Darius:
you make me a better person!

Special thanks to those who have been instrumental in my
spiritual growth, development, healing and deliverance.

To my mother, Marilyn Eldridge, former pastors, spiritual
mentors, and my dear "Sister-Friends," thank you for all that
you have imparted into my life!

To my spiritual daughter, Kay-Kay, and my future
son-in-love, Durrell Hill, thank you for loving me
as much as I love you!

FOREWORD

Dr. Veontae R. Mann

I am excited and deeply honored to write this foreword for a subject that I believe is extremely important in the body of Christ. It is a subject that is near and dear to my heart because of my own testimony. Without it, I would not be here today.

There was a time in my life when I smiled on the outside, but I was completely devastated and broken on the inside. I learned to function while wounded and bleeding. Like so many people, I wore toughness like a business suit. Unfortunately, underneath it all lay scars of rejection, guilt and shame. I experienced betrayal at the hands of someone who promised to love me forever. I battled each day to survive memories of physical violence and verbal abuse. I thank the Holy Spirit for taking me back to my upbringing and reminding me of what it means when Jesus heals and sets you free.

In a world overrun with distractions and challenges, the search for inner peace has become a necessity. I believe

Dr. Lavita S. Modest delivers an on-time masterpiece that will be a blessing to countless men and women who are seeking renewal and restoration. The Modest Model™ serves as a guide, providing direction on the concept of spiritual freedom.

> Healing and deliverance help make the masterpiece clearer.

If you are seeking wholeness, Dr. Lavita S. Modest invites you to go beyond the surface. She invites you to delve deeply into the essence of what it truly means to experience healing and deliverance with her simple seven steps. I admire how Lavita is not afraid to acknowledge our human imperfections, and our struggles, by sharing her own testimony of overcoming. She reminds us that healing and deliverance is our inheritance.

I have always believed the truth will set us free. Through our acknowledgments, this book truly confirms it. Submitting to God reveals our true purpose. Healing and deliverance help make the masterpiece clearer. Even though my story is different from Lavita's, our love for learning and teaching is the same. I am pleased to have a divine connection with the woman called "Redeemed." We walk in harmony because I too have been "Redeemed."

I believe you will receive an anointed teaching in this book. Do not be afraid to follow it and *apply* it. Make sure you share it with others who desire freedom, as well.

You will find it to be biblically sound with scholarly research. With so many untruths in the world, we desperately need God's truth. It is my belief and my sensitivity to the Holy Spirit that Dr. Lavita S. Modest possesses greatness. She will do a phenomenal job when it comes to leading the spiritual healing and deliverance initiative for the Kingdom.

All the glory belongs to Him!

PROLOGUE

The infallible Word of God is the primary source of truth. Claims of the Bible's infallibility constitutes a significant part of a Christian belief system. Furthermore, the Bible is a roadmap for the believer that provides guidance on how to live life according to the will of God. God desires for His children to be healed and delivered from all hurt, harm, and danger. The Bible allows us to hear from God and to understand His will for our lives. As such, while other resources were used to complete this book, God's Word surely can stand alone. It needs no other resource to support its claim.

In addition to using the Holy Bible as source materials, I also considered the viewpoints of other authors. Their content supports spiritual healing and deliverance. These authors also stand on the doctrine found in the Holy Bible. As such, I consider their work as reputable reference materials. Finally, the viewpoints of those authors align with my perspective and are in no way disputed.

Finally, inspired by personal experience, this book is written from a believer's point of view, using my past hurt and trauma as a guidepost on how I received healing and deliverance. The seven steps discussed in Chapter Three are actions coined from my perspective and experiences. Life experiences and examples are indeed the best teachers.

This book briefly touches on clinical mental health diagnosis, symptoms, and treatments. There are times when a person may experience clinical symptoms of illnesses, requiring clinical treatments. Some may experience spiritual conditions, which may require spiritual remedies. Then there are times when a person may experience both. As an Ordained Pastor, Clinical Mental Health Counselor, and a Doctor of Christian Counseling, I am "qualified" to treat both clinical and spiritual concerns for my clients.

TABLE OF CONTENTS

INTRODUCTION

When dealing with physical problems, such as sickness and hunger, physical remedies are possible solutions. In a similar vein, should spiritual solutions be used when confronting spiritual problems? There are times when even physical concerns may result from spiritual issues, which this book will examine. This book will also explore whether healing is achievable spiritually, emotionally, and physically, and whether it is possible to receive spiritual deliverance from generational curses (trauma), strongholds, and trouble. Additionally, if spiritual healing and deliverance are possible, what are the principal factors required to achieve spiritual healing and deliverance in the life of a believer? Set forth in this book is a seven-step model as outlined: acknowledging the need for healing and deliverance; believing that it can be achieved; confession; determination (resilience); evaluating areas that require healing and deliverance; forgiveness (of self and others) and God, who ultimately grants the gift of healing and deliverance in the life of His people.

Key terms include spiritual, emotional, physical, generational, strongholds, and trouble. For this work, the Dictionary defines spiritual as of or relating to a person's inner character.[1] Emotional is defined as having and expressing strong feelings.[2] Physical shall be anything relating to the body.[3] Generational is defined as relating to different generations, such as people or members of a family.[4] A stronghold shall be defined as a place or area where a particular belief or activity is common.[5] Trouble is defined as problems or difficulties, as well as a situation a person experiences, usually because of something they have done wrong or poorly.[6]

Spiritual healing and deliverance are topics worth investigating...

Spiritual healing and deliverance are topics worth investigating as they will help individuals achieve holistic healing from past trauma, abuse, neglect, and other psychological conditions. Once people receive the inner healing and deliverance needed, they can go on to live productive lives, live out their God-given purpose, and

---

[1] (Dictionary 2023), Spiritual
[2] (Dictionary 2023), Emotional
[3] (Dictionary 2023), Physical
[4] (Dictionary 2023), Generational
[5] (Dictionary 2023), Stronghold
[6] (Dictionary 2023), Trouble

become a testimony for others who may be suffering. This book will answer the following questions: What is spiritual healing and deliverance? If there is such a thing, how can it be achieved? What are the steps involved in achieving and maintaining healing? The scope of this work will cover not only what the Holy Bible says about spiritual healing and deliverance, but also what others have written.

This topic is presented from a theoretical, non-empirical viewpoint. Moreover, this will be explored from a Christian believer's point of view. I will not discuss non-believers, non-Christians, or other religions. The Holy Bible will be the primary source for this book, as well as what others have written and researched about the topics and from the author's personal experience.

The next chapter starts by defining healing in spiritual, emotional, and physical areas. This chapter examines how healing occurs in the mind, body, and soul. The term deliverance is defined, and generational curses (trauma), strongholds, and trouble will be explored. Chapter Two explains how past hurt and trauma are caused by each area studied, and how it impacts the overall well-being of individuals needing deliverance. We will also investigate the need for deliverance from demonic forces that require initial and ongoing deliverance. Chapter Three: *The Modest Model for Healing and Deliverance* is a theoretical approach from my perspective and introduces *The Modest Model for Healing and Deliverance*, which I developed. The model contains seven necessary steps achieve spiritual healing and deliverance. Lastly, Chapter Four: Manifestation of Healing provides a content summary and conclusion for the research outlined in this book. It demonstrates how others have received spiritual healing and deliverance and how *The Modest Model for Healing and Deliverance* can be used to achieve and maintain spiritual healing and deliverance.

WHAT IS SPIRITUAL HEALING & DELIVERANCE?
Spiritual Healing

All humans are created in the image of God[7], who is not carnal, but a spirit. Humans, who are carnal possess a spirit that is capable of being damaged. When this happens, healing must take place for that individual to move beyond the effects of the hurt. Effects such as feelings of worthlessness, brokenness, and hopelessness are caused by spiritual trauma and, thus, require spiritual healing. Spirituality is at the core of one's existence. It's the innermost part of one's being. Therefore, healing of the spirit requires inner healing. Seeing as spiritual healing deals with the inner healing of an individual, the discipline of digging deep, under the guidance of the Holy Spirit, is required to discover unpleasant roots that might be springing

> Comfort and guidance can be provided by the Holy Spirit if invited by the one in search of healing.

---

[7] (Hindson 2002), Genesis 1:27, KJV

back to life and to bring them to an effective death on the cross.[8] Digging deep requires a person to be steadfast and relentless in pursuing healing. It requires a high level of self-awareness and consciousness of their feelings.

Reliving trauma can be daunting on its face as it frequently requires a deep dive into painful experience(s). The pain of reliving trauma may cause a person to retreat prematurely and shy away from the pursuit of spiritual healing. However, comfort and guidance can be provided by the Holy Spirit if invited by the one in search of

> He can turn any tragedy into a triumph, just as He did with the death of Jesus on the cross.

healing. The Holy Spirit can remind them that Jesus died on the cross for them, which can address feelings of worthlessness, for He was broken and bruised for our transgressions.[9] Moreover, because he was bruised for our iniquities, we are already healed and can experience earthly manifestations of healing.

When dealing with feelings of hopelessness, God declares, *"For I know the plans I have for you," declares the Lord, "plans to prosper you and not to harm you, plans to give you hope and*

---

[8] (Sandford and Sandford, A Comprehensive Guide to Deliverance and Inner Healing 1998), p. 50

[9] (Hindson 2002), Isaish 53:5, KJV

a future."[10] In other words, God has a purpose and plan for our lives. He can turn any tragedy into a triumph, just as He did with the death of Jesus on the cross. In what appeared to be a hopeless and dire situation, after the crucifixion of Jesus Christ, God raised Jesus from the dead, on which one can draw hope when faced with hopeless situations. The resurrection of Jesus Christ demonstrates that God can resurrect any dead situation in the lives of His children and can change their lives instantly.

Inner healing aims to change individuals—and indeed, the entire Body of Christ—into *"a mature man to the measure of the stature which belongs to the fulness of Christ"* (Ephesians 4:13).[11] Spiritual inner healing promotes spiritual maturity that builds character and elevates knowledge in the lives of believers. Knowledge of the Son of God helps us understand that there is no pain in life that we will ever endure that Jesus did not take to the cross. There is no pain more significant than what our Lord, Jesus Christ, endured on the cross.

As heirs of God, and co-heirs with Christ, we should rejoice when we experience suffering, knowing that if we share in the suffering of Christ, we can also share in his glory.[12] Just as Jesus was physically and verbally persecuted,

[10] (Zondevan 2002), Jeremiah 29:11, NIV

[11] (Sandford and Sandford, A Comprehensive Guide to Deliverance and Inner Healing 1998), p. 53

[12] (Zondevan 2002), Romans 8:17-18, NIV

we can expect to experience the same persecution. Equally, just as Jesus overcame the trouble He experienced in the world,[13] we, too, can expect to be overcomers.[14] Spiritual healing can be accomplished in the lives of believers when we acknowledge who we are and who we were created to be: children of God and the Body of Christ. Just as the physical body of Christ was broken, buried, and risen, we, too, are broken by pain and trauma. We can rise and declare spiritual healing once we bury the pain of spiritual hurt.

Spiritual

Our spirituality evolves from our internal character traits received from the Spirit of God at birth. As we age and mature, our individual characteristics are developed out of our feelings and they impact, if not dictate, our actions and behaviors. We can experience spiritual healing by addressing our maladaptive feelings and actions. Our spirit, according to the Word of God, is capable of experiencing and expressing many things: troubledness (John 13:21), distress (Acts 17:16), fear (Romans 8:16) and longing (Isaiah 26:9). Our spirit testifies (Romans 8:16), prays (1 Corinthians 14:14), sings (1 Corinthians 14:15), praises (1 Corinthians 14:16), tends toward envy (James 4:5), expresses faithfulness or unfaithfulness (Psalm 78:8), and worships

---

[13] (Zondevan 2002), John 16:33, NIV
[14] (Zondevan 2002), 1 John 5:4, NIV

(John 4:23).[15] Feelings of troubledness, distress, fear, anxiety, anger, shame, and longing are among those that would require spiritual healing. Scripture addresses these emotions and provides us with remedies to heal and remediate feelings contrary to God's will and purpose for our lives.

Biblical Remedies for Anxiety, Anger & Shame

The Bible contains Scriptures that are applicable when confronted with anxiety, anger, and shame. The simple uncertainties of life can cause anxiety, much less anyone living under impoverished conditions, or income and food insecurity. Students may suffer from test anxiety during an academic examination. However, when

> ...while life may be uncertain to us, the Creator of the universe knows how life turns out...

faced with anxiety, the Bible exhorts us, *"Be anxious for nothing, but in everything, by prayer and supplication, with thanksgiving, let your requests be made known to God."*[16] Worrying is worthless. It's counterproductive to the will of God. Understanding that while life may be uncertain to us, the Creator of the universe knows how life turns out for

---

[15] (Sandford and Sandford, Healing the Wounded Spirit 1985), p.29
[16] (Zondevan 2002), Philippians 4:6, NIV

His children. As with any good father, God only wants the best for us. We can relax and have peace in this promise.

A person dealing with anger could benefit from practicing breathing techniques, guided imagery, or progressive muscle relaxation ...

The story of Cain and Abel quickly comes to mind when discussing anger. Cain's anger against his brother, Abel, led to murder.[17] Unfortunately, this level of anger and rage still holds true today. Murder and assaults are still conducted because of one's inability to channel anger. Individuals dealing with anger issues are like ticking time bombs waiting to explode. When experiencing anger, Ecclesiastes 7:9 exhorts us, *"Do not be quickly provoked in your spirit, for anger resides in the lap of fools."*[18] Anger management techniques could help manage unwarranted anger. A person dealing with anger could benefit from practicing breathing techniques, guided imagery, or progressive muscle relaxation to eliminate symptoms of anger. These techniques could shield them from becoming easily provoked and from committing shameful acts that they will eventually regret at a minimum, if they do not lose their freedom at most.

---

[17] (Zondevan 2002), Genesis 4:5-8, NIV
[18] (Zondevan 2002), Ecclesiastes 7:9, NIV

King David was no stranger to shame. He prayed to God and asked to be delivered from blood guilt after the murder of Urah.[19] He was filled with guilt, which prompted him to pray. Shame produces an overwhelming embarrassment and humiliation from having done something dishonorable. Adam and Eve tried to hide from God in the Garden of Eden because they were ashamed.[20] Instead of hiding, we should humble ourselves and ask God to help us.

Humbling oneself before God is the first step to overcoming shame. When feeling ashamed, 1 Peter 4:16 says, *"However, if you suffer as a Christian, do not be ashamed, but praise God that you bear that name."*[21] As Christians, we should consider the shame that Jesus endured and expect to experience shame in this lifetime. Shame shows up in various ways. One may experience shame from their own actions or the actions of others. Unfortunately, people are ashamed when they become victims of domestic violence, rape, molestation, schemes, and evil actions committed by others. Whether we experience shame from our own actions, or the actions of others, we can look to Jesus for comfort.

The Apostle Peter says that when we suffer, we should do it in a way that glorifies God. When we experience the shame of betrayal, divorce, becoming financially depleted or

---

[19] (Zondevan 2002), Psalm 51:14, NIV
[20] (Zondevan 2002), Genesis 3:8, NIV
[21] (Zondevan 2002), 1 Peter 4:16, NIV

a battered spouse, we can look to Jesus as a model for how He endured a public display of shame on the cross. Jesus knew He would soon be His Father's right hand–in the presence of His heavenly Father. Whenever we experience shame, we can praise God that we are in His presence and can find healing and deliverance from any shameful situation. The presence of God found in Scripture provides a haven and refuge from unwanted feelings and emotions.

Scripture not only addresses feelings that we may experience, but it also provides actions necessary to promote spiritual healing. When we pray, with the help of the Holy Spirit who helps us in our weakness, *"the Spirit himself intercedes for us through wordless groans."*[22] Moreover, *"he who searches our hearts knows the mind of the Spirit because the Spirit intercedes with God's people in accordance with the will of God."*[23] Seeing that it is God's will that we are healed when we pray, we can have the things we ask for in prayer.[24] When we praise God, we are reminded of his presence, *"Surely the righteous will praise your name, and the upright will live in your presence."*[25] In the presence of God, we can have everything we need, including spiritual healing.

---

[22] (Zondevan 2002), Romans 8:26, NIV
[23] (Zondevan 2002), Romans 8:27, NIV
[24] (Zondevan 2002), Mark 11:24, NIV
[25] (Zondevan 2002), Psalm 140:13, NIV

Emotional

Emotional healing takes place when, regardless of one's circumstances, mood, or relationships with others, one can experience real peace and joy through a relationship with Jesus Christ. Experiencing adverse circumstances may cause one to bear emotions such as fear, disgust, depression, and disappointment. These emotions can be exceedingly difficult to overcome, but can be achieved, resulting in emotional healing. Practicing mindfulness is essential when facing adverse emotions. As defined in the Cambridge Dictionary, mindfulness is the practice of being aware of your body, mind, and feelings, in the

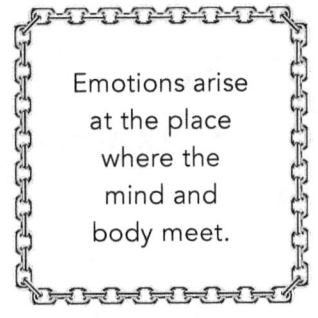

Emotions arise at the place where the mind and body meet.

present moment, thought to create a feeling of calm.[26] Before one can put a "fix" in place to any problem or malfunction, is ascertaining the source of the problem not a prerequisite? The same principle applies when people need to overcome adversity or negative emotions. This heightened sense of awareness is used to identify triggers that cause negative emotions. With this information, one becomes better equipped to act or respond differently when confronted by triggers.

---

[26] (Dictionary 2023), Mindfulness

Emotions arise at the place where the mind and body meet. It is the body's reaction to the mind—or, say, a reflection of the mind in the body.[27] Emotions cause a person to respond or react to what they are feeling. For example, if a person is angry, they may lash out at other individuals. Similarly, if a person is embarrassed, they may withdraw from social activities. Emotions, such as fear, may limit one's ability to try new things, go to

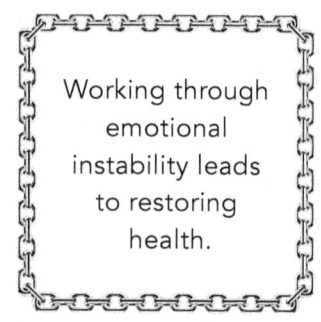

Working through emotional instability leads to restoring health.

unfamiliar places, or pursue dreams and desires. Although they may want to try new things, they are frozen in fear.

Four Major Emotions: Anxiety, Fear, Anger & Guilt

Whether we suffer from neurosis, or common fears such as a fear of people or a fear of our feelings, we can begin to heal those areas by working through the four emotions of anxiety, fear, anger, and guilt. Like other emotions, these feelings are neither good nor bad in themselves. However, when these four emotions are buried, it can lead to emotional instability. Working through emotional instability

---

[27] (Tolle 1999), p.25

leads to restoring health.[28] Having an awareness of emotional dysregulation is the start to achieving wellness.

The first emotion, anxiety, may cause one to have excessive, uncontrollable worry, feeling a loss of control, and an inability to concentrate. There are different symptoms associated with anxiety, and there are a variety of anxiety disorders, Such as Social Anxiety Disorder, Panic Disorder, and Generalized Anxiety Disorder to name a few.

A person suffering from Social Anxiety Disorder may experience fears that he or she will act in a way or show anxiety symptoms that will be negatively evaluated by others, causing them to be humiliated or embarrassed, or feelings of rejection by others.[29] Social anxiety can cause a person to become distant and isolate themselves from others, causing them to feel lonely, depressed, and even suicidal.

A person who has panic disorder may experience physical responses of a pounding heart, sweating, and choking. This type of panic promotes fear of losing control or even dying.[30] Symptoms of panic disorders feel like overwhelming fear, shutting down a person's ability to react and respond appropriately to frightening situations. Fortunately, panic disorders are treatable with a variety of

---

[28] (Linn and Linn, Healing Memories Through the Five Stages of Forgiveness 1977), p.24
[29] (APA 2022), p. 229
[30] (APA 2022), p. 235-236

therapy options. Prayer is the most effective treatment option of them all.

Generalized Anxiety Disorder occurs when a person has excessive anxiety and worry, and the individual finds it difficult to control their worrying. They may have symptoms of restlessness, being easily fatigued, irritability, muscle tension, and sleep disturbance.[31] Anxiety and panic can trigger a person to retreat into a shell for fear of when it may arise, especially in public. There are other anxiety disorders wherein a person struggles with managing responsibilities in their day-to-day lives. When these symptoms are treated, the person can return to a normal level of functioning or at least minimize the effects of anxiety.

The Bible addresses anxiety in 1 Peter 5:7, which states, *"Cast all your anxiety on Him, because He cares for you."*[32] God, being omniscient, knew there would be anxiety-provoking situations we would face in life. So, He provided instructions on how to manage anxiety and worry. Knowing that worrying does not add one day to our lives,[33] we are blessed to have access to God, who can change the universe with the blink of an eye. We can find comfort from symptoms of anxiety by knowing God recognizes and cares about us and our situations that create anxiety.

---

[31] (APA 2022), p. 250
[32] (Zondervan 1989), 1 Peter 5:7, NRSV
[33] (Zondervan 1989), Mark 12:25, NRSV

The second emotion, fear, is a common, unpleasant emotion that can be paralyzing. Fear can be rational and irrational. Irrational fears require emotional healing as it prevents people from achieving their God-ordained destiny. Most fears are learned behaviors. For example, children are typically fearless due to their level of

Most fears are learned behaviors. For example, children are typically fearless due to their level of immaturity.

immaturity. However, as they mature and become more knowledgeable of the world and the things in it, that innocent fearlessness starts to subside.

Fear and phobias are close relatives; they both can interfere with a person's ability to fulfill the responsibilities of a customary day. While closely related, they differ in intensity. Someone with a fear of riding in an elevator may be able to manage riding in one when necessary. In contrast, someone with a phobia of riding in elevators must opt to take the stairs instead or look for another alternative altogether. Humans are born with an innate sense of fear, which aids in protecting us from harm when faced with actual and imminent danger. In contrast, a phobia is an excessive fear or anxiety related to specific objects or situations that are out of proportion to the actual danger posed by the object or situation.[34]

---

[34] (Hull 2022), Fear vs. Phobia: What is the Difference

As previously stated, fear can be rational or irrational. Irrational fear is a tactic of the enemy used to keep a person from experiencing life the way God has designed. The enemy comes to steal, kill, and destroy,[35] and

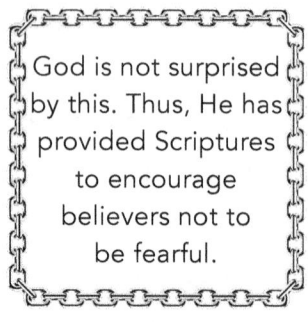

God is not surprised by this. Thus, He has provided Scriptures to encourage believers not to be fearful.

fear is one of the weapons he employs to steal freedom, kill dreams, and destroy destinies. God is not surprised by this. Thus, He has provided Scriptures to encourage believers not to be fearful. Passages, such as Isaiah 41:10, tells us not to be afraid because God is with us and will strengthen us.[36] Furthermore, God did not give us a spirit of fear,[37] so we know that fear is not of God. Therefore, it is of our adversary, Satan. We can trust that the adversary is defeated because if God is for us, who can be against us?[38]

Like fear, the third emotion, anger has many variations. According to the *Diagnostic and Statistical Manual of Mental Disorders: DSM 5-TR*, anger is a crucial criterion in clinical mental health diagnosis, including Intermittent Explosive Disorder, Oppositional Defiant Disorder, Disruptive Mood Dysregulation Disorder, Borderline Personality Disorder,

---

[35] (Zondervan 2002), John 10:10, NIV

[36] (Zondervan 2002), Isaiah 41:10, NIV

[37] (Zondervan 2002), 2 Timothy 1:7, NIV

[38] (Zondevan 2002), Romans 8:31 NIV

and Bipolar Personality Disorder. Anger is displayed through verbal and physical behaviors. It can be directed toward people, animals, and/or objects. Someone dealing with excessive, unwarranted anger might display temper tantrums, temper outbursts, and pronounced aggression. People with anger management issues are generally easily provoked and said to have a short fuse. It is the intensity of one's anger that indicates the type of anger a person may be experiencing.

Anger can also be learned behavior. For instance, a child witnessing a parent's continual inability to regulate their temper may in turn adopt the same maladaptive responses to situations when confronted with frustrating circumstances. Anger can also be the reaction to, or means of coping with, an inner suffering that a person may experience. Healing and deliverance of the core concern will be necessary to properly process the feelings of anger, aggression, and rage. Unfortunately, healing and deliverance may not come expeditiously. It could take time and deep soul searching. This is especially true if the individual cannot pinpoint the cause or source of their anger due to unresolved grief or adverse childhood experiences. Inner suffering can be so deeply suppressed and inaccessible to the person. This will greatly impede one's ability to remedy or resolve the negative impact of past trauma or hurt.

Anger is typically a signal that one disagrees with something in their life. While anger is not necessarily a terrible thing, unresolved anger that leads to sin is prohibited in the Bible. *"In your anger, do not sin. Do not let the sun go down while you are still angry, and do not give the devil a foothold."*[39] In other words, we should do whatever is necessary, within a timely manner, to address the cause of anger. Allowing time to lapse affords the devil the opportunity to wreak havoc in the person's life and relationships with others. It also allows a person time to ruminate, rehearse, and misinterpret communications, which often worsens the situation. Even when anger is warranted, there are ways to effectively navigate situations without having temper tantrums, responding in rage, or doing something a person may regret in the future, potentially causing them to live with shame and guilt unnecessarily. Some ways include taking a break, counting, or taking deep breaths to calm down and refocus. When all else fails, pray.

The fourth emotion, guilt, can be an unbearable burden to carry. In fact, many succumb to the effects caused by guilt. Guilt could come from offenses committed by the one in need of healing, or from the actions of others. While the weight of guilt may be soul-crushing, the Bible contains

---

[39] (Zondervan 2002), Ephesians 4:26-27, NIV

Verbal abuse is a caustic and demeaning language when communicating...

passages of Scripture to help one heal from feelings of guilt. Passages include Hebrews 10:22, which states, *"Let us draw near to God with a sincere heart and with the full assurance that faith brings, having our hearts sprinkled to cleanse us from a guilty conscience and having our bodies washed with pure waters."*[40] This passage helps us understand that we can be cleansed from having a guilty conscience when we cultivate a relationship with God through our Christian disciplines of prayer, praise, and worship. The cleansing received from God brings about an emotional catharsis and healing in the lives of believers who bear the burden of emotional baggage.

Another type of emotional hurt is verbal abuse, which is a form of psychological/emotional abuse. Verbal abuse is a caustic and demeaning language when communicating with a spouse, child, or elderly person. It is typically used by caregivers or other people in a position of power. Examples of verbal abuse include name-calling, belittling, and derogatory and critical remarks.[41] This type of abuse can leave a long-lasting mark on the person on the receiving end and can be just as detrimental as physical abuse. Emotional

---

[40] (Zondervan 2002), Hebrews 10:22, NIV
[41] (M. Morgan 2019), p. 21

abuse can take a severe toll on a person's overall well-being and can significantly damage their self-image. The damage caused by long sustained verbal abuse requires healing.

A poor self-image can be the result of verbal abuse, and the Bible contains Scripture for dealing with the damage. Ephesians 4:24 says, *"and put on the new self, created to be like God in true righteousness and holiness."*[42], and Colossians 3:10 says, *"and have put on the new self, which is being renewed in knowledge in the image of its Creator."*[43] These verses, when meditated on, can provide healing for someone suffering from poor self-image. It can help restore their confidence, understanding that we have been made in the image of the One who is incapable of error.

The healing that can be provided by the Word of God is not limited to this body of work. Emotions such as sadness, disappointment, bitterness, and jealousy are all susceptible to healing made available through God's Word. The Word of God gives hope to anyone in need of emotional healing. It contains appendages with topics and

Holding unforgiving thoughts in our minds can negatively impact our well-being.

---

[42] (Zondervan 2002), Ephesians 4:24, NIV
[43] (Zondervan 2002), Colossians: 3:10, NIV

Scripture—far too many to list,—that address every emotional situation.

Physical

Physical abuse can happen to both children and adults of either gender or any sexual orientation. The injuries can be inflicted by punching, kicking, biting, burning, or use of a weapon. Physical abuse can result in bruises, burns, poisoning, broken bones, and internal hemorrhages.[44] Physical abuse is any action that intentionally harms or injures another person. While physical wounds may heal naturally, the mental impact can be long-lasting for the person suffering from abuse.

By law, pharmaceutical companies must disclose all potential side effects of prescription drugs. Would you agree that most people would avoid taking drugs with known detrimental side effects? Unfortunately, we are not as discerning about the detrimental thoughts we put in our minds, nor are we aware of the toxic effects these thoughts can have on our bodies.[45] Holding unforgiving thoughts in our minds can negatively impact our well-being. Headaches, backaches, pains in the neck, stomachaches and ulcer-like symptoms, depression, lack of energy, anxiety, irritability,

---

[44] (M. Morgan 2019), p. 22
[45] (Jampolsky, M.D. 1999), p. 25

tenseness and being "on edge," insomnia, and restlessness are all physical problems that may be associated with an unforgiving mind.[46]

Research shows that nonphysical things like thoughts and emotions affect our bodies at the cellular level, just as surely as genes, lifestyle or the medicines we take. Emotions—particularly depression and stress—are linked to heart attacks.[47] Feelings of guilt may cause a person to experience physical manifestations. The body loses its vitality, energy, and enthusiasm.[48] These physical ailments resulting from maladaptive beliefs or thoughts further demonstrate the mind-body connection.

The mind and body connection informs people when they must perform voluntary and involuntary activities, such as sleeping and eating. It is astonishing how psychological problems impact sleep, appetite, touch, digestion, and arousal.[49] A person suffering from symptoms of anxiety or trauma may notice a decrease in their appetite for food or may have trouble sleeping. A person suffering from sexual abuse may have difficulties with arousal. Collaborating with a licensed professional therapist may be required to assist

---

[46] (Jampolsky, M.D. 1999), p.30-31
[47] (Bradley Hagerty 2009), p. 50
[48] (Fleagle 2022), p. 74
[49] (Van Der Kolk, M.D. 2014), p. 56

the person with overcoming the mental health issues that manifest in physical ailments.

Deliverance

Since the beginning of time, there was One who could deliver people from sickness, burdens, enemies, and more. God is our G.O.D. (giver of deliverance)! King David praises God in Psalm 40:17, saying, *As for me, I am poor and needy, but the Lord takes thought for me. You are my help and my deliverer; do not delay, O my God.*[50] The poor

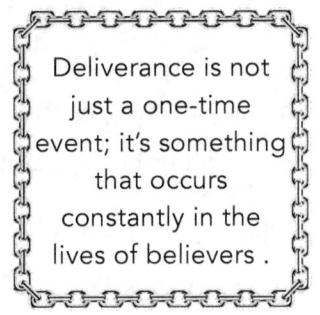

Deliverance is not just a one-time event; it's something that occurs constantly in the lives of believers .

and needy have a special place in God's heart. He cares for them and is ready to deliver them from burdens. God can set one free from bondage—the bondage of generational curses, poor patterns of thinking or strongholds, and even life's everyday troubles. Deliverance is not just a one-time event; it's something that occurs constantly in the lives of believers. Deliverance from the bondage of generational trauma/curses, strongholds, and trouble is no easy task. It requires commitment, consistency, and communication with the One who can deliver us from any situation: God!

---

[50] (Zondervan 1989), Psalm 40:17

Generational Curses (Trauma)

Although Adam was the first man God created, it was never His intent for only Adam to know His love and teachings. It was for generations to come. Generations are essential to God, according to the Holy Bible. Genesis 17:7 states, *"I will establish my covenant as an everlasting covenant between me and you and your descendants after you for generations to come, to be your God and the God of your descendants after you."*[51] God intends for each generation to teach their children about Him and keep His commandments.[52]

The word "generation" is mentioned more than seven hundred times in Scripture.[53] In Scripture, 1,314 passages speak about parents and children, 2,208 verses concern a father's relationship with his son, and 1,426 passages instruct fathers.[54] The portion of Scripture that deals with passing the torch from one generation to the following total 180.[55] As with all other matters dear to God, they are threats to the enemy who will attempt to infiltrate the generational bloodline through evil deeds, behaviors, and

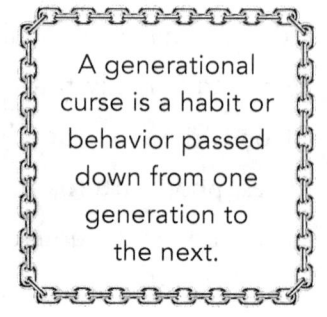

A generational curse is a habit or behavior passed down from one generation to the next.

---

[51] (Zondevan 2002), Genesis 17:7, NIV

[52] (Zondevan 2002), Deuteronomy 11:18-19, NRSV

[53] (Nori 2005), p. 16

[54] (Nori 2005), p. 17

[55] (Nori 2005), p. 17

mindsets to thwart God's will for many generations. If the enemy is victorious, many say that families may struggle under a generational curse.

A generational curse is a habit or behavior passed down from one generation to the next. Generational curses result from the iniquities of the former generations and generally come to us in three ways.[56] The first way is through our genetic inheritance of propensities to sin.[57] For example, the genetics of a person may predispose them to alcoholism or drug addiction if their parent(s) used alcohol or drugs during the pregnancy. There is a high chance the person is subject to becoming an alcoholic through the inheritance of the generational sins of their parents.

Illnesses passed down through the bloodline, creating sickness and diseases, can also create generational curses passed down to other generations. For this reason, doctors usually conduct a family medical history to determine if their patients have any family bloodline illnesses. Diseases such as cancer, heart disease, diabetes, and high blood pressure are all examples of illnesses that can be passed down genetically.

A second means of passing trauma from one generation to another is by way of example, as children commonly

---

[56] (Zondervan 2002), Exodus
[57] (Sandford and Sandford, Healing the Wounded Spirit 1985), p.371

mimic their parents' behavior, whether good or bad. As a result, children learn to become what the parents are rather than what they teach.[58] The commonality of this type of inconsistency is that the cliché, "Do as I say, not as I do!" evolved. When there is a stark contrast in a parent's behavior from what the parent instructs the child, confusion naturally arises for the child. So, instead of "doing" as instructed, they mimic what they see. For example, suppose a parent uses foul language regularly. In that case, the child may use the same language based on what they have heard from their parents.

Generational curses descend to future generations through words, as words are powerful. Words are seeds planted in the minds and hearts of children. They can be both helpful and harmful in their development. Children's earliest opinions of themselves develop from words spoken to them or over them. Unfortunately, parents sometimes talk to their children out of pain and anger. They say the exact hurtful words to their children spoken to them by their parents, intentionally or unintentionally.[59] This could result from familiar spirits working through the family bloodline. For instance, an abused child will likely grow into an abusive adult toward their children, perhaps speaking word curses to their children. Words such as, "You are dumb," "You are

---

[58] (Sandford and Sandford, Healing the Wounded Spirit 1985), p.379
[59] (Nori 2005), p. 22

stupid," or "You are just like your drunk father" are curses that a person tends to believe. This ultimately dictates how they think, organize, and process information about their environment and the world around them.

Sowing and reaping is the third method of generational trauma that descends to future generations.[60] A person can expect to receive, as a harvest, whatever they plant in life as defined by the biblical principle of sowing and reaping.[61] This biblical principle of sowing and reaping warns against overt sins and

Sowing and reaping evil is the result of overt sin.

forbidden rituals to avoid spiritual attacks in the form of demonic oppression.

Sowing and reaping evil is the result of overt sin. Examples of overt sins might include constant viewing of pornography, repetitive lying, slander, or rebellion. Any of these might provide an open door to demonic oppression.[62] Generational sowing and reaping of curses stem from learned behavior in the household. Forbidden rituals, such as idol worship, practiced in the home become part of the child's behavior, creating an attachment to the family curses. Demonic intrusion may manifest in the form of

---

[60] (Sandford and Sandford, Healing the Wounded Spirit 1985), p. 379

[61] (Zondevan 2002), Galatians 6:7, NIV

[62] (Harrigton and Harrington 2011), p.47

impure spirits, creating cravings for defiled things, such as addiction to gambling, perverse sexual fetishes, or drugs and alcohol. It could also manifest in the form of depression, chronic fear, other compulsive behaviors, violence, or even self-harm.

A person suffering from generational curses, whether through genetics or actions, may find healing and deliverance through repentance and the blood of Jesus Christ. While repentance from occult activity begins the healing process, it only removes the iniquity from us, but not the demons associated with it. Neither will it close the door that we have opened to demonic intrusion. We must aggressively cast out whatever demonic beings we let in and renounce our involvement to shut off further access.[63]

> The blood of Jesus Christ is the only effective weapon in such an attack on the family bloodline.

Demons are relentless and do not easily give up. The Bible declares, "*Once an unclean spirit has gone out of a person, it may only leave for a period but return with even more unclean spirits*"[64] to wreak havoc in the person's life. This pattern of demonic intrusion explains why relapse is quite common for someone who may be struggling with addictions. The person

---

[63] (Harrigton and Harrington 2011), p.44
[64] (Zondervan 2002), Matthew 12:43-44, NIV

may seem to be free from the addiction(s) for a period but later seems to be doing worse.[65]

The repeated pattern of spiritual attacks present along generational bloodlines is more challenging to break because they are deep-seated and rooted attacks on the family line. The blood of Jesus Christ is the only effective weapon in such an attack on the family bloodline. His blood is powerful enough to break and destroy any generational curse. Christians have the authority to declare victory against any demonic intrusion by pronouncing the blood of Jesus over every situation.

While generational curses may be consequences of our sins, or the enemy's work that may affect future generations, God's grace and mercy offer a solution and redemption from the curse(s). God's foolproof solution was accomplished on the cross at Calvary when He sent His Son to become a ransom for many, providing healing and redemption for future generations.[66] Jesus died for our sins; therefore, we are no longer slaves to sin;[67] instead, we receive adoption into the bloodline and family of God as heirs with God and co-heirs with Christ.[68]

---

[65] (Zondevan 2002), Matthew 12:45, NIV
[66] (Zondervan 1989), Mark 10:45 NRVS
[67] (Zondervan 1989), Romans 6:6, NRVS
[68] (Zondervan 1989), Romans 8:14-17, NRVS

Through our adoption, we are set free from the generational curses of our biological families. The negative generational character traits are replaced with our actual image[69]—the image of God in which we were created. We have a generational connection to our Lord and Savior, Jesus Christ, as we were created in His image and possess His spirit. The connection with Christ severs the connections of our biological, sinful families. Freedom from biological family curses occurs when we accept Jesus as our Savior and enter right standing with God.[70] Whatever sins and sin natures that have not come to the cross within the family history can serve as points of access and control for demonic forces[71] and manifest as generational trauma/curses. In addition to repentance and the blood of Jesus, healing and deliverance from the generational curse(s) may require counseling, praying, and fasting for the person(s) affected by sin in the bloodline.

Strongholds

As previously stated, a stronghold is defined as a place or area where a particular belief or activity is common.[72] Strongholds are a significant contributor to sin and sinful

---

[69] (Zondervan 2002), Genesis 1:27, NIV

[70] (Zondevan 2002), Roman 3:22, NIV

[71] (Sandford and Sandford, A Comprehensive Guide to Deliverance and Inner Healing 1998), p.31

[72] (Dictionary 2023), Stronghold

natures, which we have the power to demolish. We have spent our whole lives acquiring various attitudes and behaviors, some good and some quite destructive to ourselves and others.[73] Some of the most apparent strongholds manifest as wrong attitudes, thinking patterns, ideas, desires, and beliefs.

One's attitude dictates how one communicates with others, conducts one's responsibilities, and impacts one's environment. Essentially, one's attitude shapes their success and happiness. Attitudes can be either positive or negative. Positive attitudes in life yield favorable results. Adversely, the stronghold of a negative attitude will directly impact a person's ability to find satisfaction in life. The stronghold of a negative attitude can have detrimental effects on the individual and those around them.

Possessing a pessimistic attitude can cause a person to drown in despair and prevent them from seeing the good in any situation. Gloom and doom shall follow them, leading to adverse personal, school, work, and social outcomes. People with a negative attitude might not see themselves as worthy enough to have good things and exaggerate

> Patterns of wrong thinking could come from broken molds that a person may have inherited from earlier generations.

[73] (Savard 1998), p.7

even the most minor things by imagining the worst possible outcome. People can rid themselves of negative attitudes by practicing positive thoughts, trying to live in the moment, acknowledging the good around them, and avoiding negative people who may influence their thinking and behavior.

In addition to having strongholds of wrong attitudes, a person can have wrong thinking patterns. The word "pattern" has many meanings, but one of its most unusual meanings best describes the "wrong patterns of thinking." Pattern means, among other things, the model used to make a mold into which molten metal is poured to

> People will assess the world around them based on their experiences from those wrong thinking patterns.

form a casting.[74] Patterns of wrong thinking could come from broken molds that a person may have inherited from earlier generations. These wrong thinking patterns may manifest as unrealistic expectations of self and others, incorrect assumptions, and the denial of reality. Patterns of thinking or the act of thinking dictate what we believe about ourselves, others, and the world around us.

The act of thinking is how we form thoughts in our minds. When mindsets (patterns of thinking) are locked into our minds, thoughts will come out of that pattern

---

[74] (Savard 1998), p.88

(mindset/mold) rigidly formed the same way every time.[75] Because it is a pattern from a particular mold, the thoughts that surface from the pattern are consistently correct, incorrect, positive, or negative. People will assess the world around them based on their experiences from those wrong thinking patterns. Some people have been badly mistreated, and their pattern of thinking receives and molds all input from others as attacks and abuse.[76] They perceive that every encounter with others will be like what they experienced through abuse.

Anyone repeatedly told they are stupid, ugly, worthless, or a failure will invariably develop patterns of wrong thinking.[77] Their wrong thinking pattern was formed out of repetition and therefore becomes their mold of thinking. Furthermore, their thoughts dictate their actions, resulting in wrong actions and behaviors. When dealing with wrong thinking patterns, healing, and deliverance can be challenging. When people change their thinking patterns, they can modify their thinking mold and achieve healing and deliverance from the impacts of wrong thinking patterns. Until the wrong thinking patterns are modified, people will have strongholds of wrong ideas.

---

[75] (Savard 1998), p.88
[76] (Savard 1998), p.88
[77] (Savard 1998), p.89

Ideas represent thoughts on a given subject.[78] Wrong ideas lead to making mistakes and bad decisions. The Bible instructs us to cast down evil imaginations, wrong theories, reasonings, and thoughts.[79] Having strongholds of wrong attitudes, wrong patterns of thinking, and wrong ideas leads to having wrong desires. Desire

Having wrong desires can harm one's mental and physical well-being.

can be a longing for something good, such as a deeper relationship with Jesus Christ.[80] However, a wrong desire can be covetousness, self-gratification, or self-indulgence.[81] Having wrong desires can harm one's mental and physical well-being.

People struggling with wrong desires may walk according to the flesh, not the Spirit. The flesh and the Spirit are contrary to one another. When dealing with wrong desires, only the flesh is being gratified.[82] Wrong desires are acts of the flesh prohibited in Galatians 5:19-21, *"The acts of the flesh are obvious: sexual immorality, impurity, and debauchery; idolatry and witchcraft; hatred, discord, jealousy, fits of rage, selfish ambition, dissensions, factions, and envy; drunkenness,*

---

[78] (Savard 1998), p.91
[79] (Savard 1998), p.91
[80] (Savard 1998), p.92
[81] (Savard 1998), p.92
[82] (Zondevan 2002), Galatians 5:16-17, NIV

orgies, and the like. I warn you, as I did before, that those who live like this will not inherit the kingdom of God."[83] Wrong desires destroy the believer's life, marriages, finances and health. Wrong desires are the root of grief and sorrow in this world, including adultery, stealing, and substance abuse.[84]

Strongholds of wrong beliefs are just as paralyzing as the others mentioned. A belief is the mental acceptance of something deserving of confidence and trust.[85] When confidence and trust in wrong beliefs occur, a Christian may have a distorted perception of "truth."[86] They may have a distorted view of themselves based on what others have told them. Additionally, they may have feelings of guilt and shame over their past, which leads them to have wrong beliefs about their future.

Fortunately, there is relief for anyone suffering with strongholds associated with the old sinful nature. Crucifying our old sinful nature helps to demolish our strongholds. According to 2 Corinthians 10:4-5, *"The weapons we fight with are not the weapons of the world. On the contrary, they have the divine power to demolish strongholds. We demolish arguments and every pretension that sets itself up against the knowledge of God, and we take captive every thought to make*

---

[83] (Zondevan 2002), Galatians 5:19-21, NIV
[84] (Savard 1998), p.93
[85] (Savard 1998), p.93
[86] (Savard 1998), p.93

it obedient to Christ."[87] Christians accomplish this to a degree by giving up the apparent things. Generally, external actions and behaviors include drinking, smoking, cursing, gambling, drugs, and fornication, which are the most apparent things most new Christians first learn to crucify.[88] In addition to addressing external actions, the key to receiving renewal as fast as possible is to tear down the strongholds around wrong mindsets.[89]

The strongholds of wrong attitudes, patterns of thinking, ideas, desires, and beliefs can be corrected when we apply the right attitudes found in the fruit of the Spirit found in Galatians 5:22-23, *"But the fruit of the Spirit is love, joy, peace, forbearance, kindness, goodness, faithfulness, gentleness, and self-control."*[90] The fruit of the Spirit and the flesh cannot cohabit because love, unforgiveness, bitterness, and kindness cannot reside in the same space. When the fruit of the Spirit is actively present in our lives, it helps to eliminate strongholds.

Christians should first bind themselves to the truth. They then need to loose any deceptions the enemy has brought to them, all wrong beliefs, and any strongholds associated with them.[91] They must subscribe to the truth in the Word

---

[87] (Zondevan 2002), 2 Corinthians 10:4-5, NIV
[88] (Savard 1998), p.86
[89] (Savard 1998), p.7
[90] (Zondevan 2002), Galatians 5:22-23, NIV
[91] (Savard 1998), p.94

of God and reject lies from the enemy. Jesus is the way, the truth, and the life.[92] When forming our beliefs, we should listen to the voice of Jesus. Christians should know His voice and follow him only.[93] Regardless of what the

The world has enormous trouble, which should be no surprise.

enemy screams, the whisper of God is more powerful and should be our source of truth. The truth of God should be the foundation on which we build our belief system.

Trouble

As stated in the introduction, trouble is defined as problems or difficulties, as well as a situation a person experiences, usually because of something they have done wrong or poorly.[94] The world has enormous trouble, which should be no surprise. After all, Jesus warned his followers in John 16:33 to expect trouble in the world. He said, *"I have told you these things so that in me you may have peace. In this world, you will have trouble. But take heart! I have overcome the world."*[95] Trouble may be the result of poverty, self-perpetuating cycles, and the evil plans of Satan.

---

[92] (Zondervan 2002), John 14:6, NIV

[93] (Zondevan 2002), John 10:27, NIV

[94] (Dictionary 2023), Trouble

[95] (Zondevan 2002), John 16:33, NIV

Poverty and poor nutrition contribute to early school dropouts and conduct problems, which limit job opportunities and feed back into the ongoing cycle of poverty.[96] Early on, human resilience research focused primarily on the problems likely to impede long-term development: poverty, chronic maltreatment, or deprivation.[97] The deprivation of vital resources, such as food and healthcare, can lead to a person experiencing trouble with their health.

One broken link in the chains of life causes others to break. When this happens, there is a trickle-down effect, causing one to spiral into the pits of trouble and despair. People who suffer from poverty may have challenges in their relationships with others, primarily due to the lack of education and the ability to communicate with others. Parents may, in turn, be abusive to their children due to their lack of knowledge and understanding of the negative impacts their behavior will have on their children. As such, maltreatment and abuse can devastate a young child's view of the world and their sense of self-esteem and trust. These deficits can then lead to

> Families often experience poverty and the fallout of poverty due to the lack of necessary resources.

---

[96] (Bonanno 2021), p.42
[97] (Bonanno 2021), p.42

social withdrawal, isolation, or violent and reckless behavior, which often leads to further victimization and self-harm later in life.[98] Until the power of poverty is broken, there is a repeated cycle of deficits, abuse, hopelessness, and misery in the family line.

Families often experience poverty and the fallout of poverty due to the lack of necessary resources. This repeated cycle continues until someone consciously decides to break the cycle and do better. Celebrities often share their testimonies of transitioning from extremely poor to prosperous conditions. The success is usually attributed to their decision to do something different than what was done in their family, like getting an education or not becoming addicted to drugs and alcohol.

While not all trouble in life is the result of Satan's work, a great deal of it is part of his evil plan to destroy lives. Evil works to delude and kill as many in its path as it wants dominion. Satan, as the ruler of the world's kingdom, seeks all of us as servants, whether as intentional slaves of darkness or unwitting sycophants.[99] He seeks to create conflict, sickness, war, and other calamities to ruin lives. Fortunately, Satan is a defeated foe! Christians have an Advocate to come to our defense in times of trouble.

---

[98] (Bonanno 2021), p.42
[99] (Allender, PhD. 1999), p. 75

In times of trouble, we can find peace with Jesus Christ by focusing on Him.[100] Trouble can cause one to be fretful and confused. However, *"the peace of God, which transcends all understanding, will guard one's hearts and minds in Christ Jesus."*[101] If people see their troubles as nothing more than isolated hassles and hurts, they will grow bitter and angry. On the contrary, if they see them as tests God uses for His glory and their development, then even the most minor incidents are significant.[102] From the Bible, we learn that God works in all things,[103] which means He is at work during trouble, and He is present with us when we are in trouble.[104] God never sleeps nor slumbers. He is always fully aware. He can work all things out for our good. God can turn a life-altering tragedy into a life-changing triumph! On the bright side, the one good thing about trouble is that it only lasts temporarily.[105] Although it may seem to go on and on, and seem never-ending, trouble eventually ends.

[100] (Zondevan 2002), Isaiah 26:3, NIV

[101] (Zondevan 2002), Philippians 4:7, NIV

[102] (Lucado, You'll Get Through This: Hope and Help for Your Turbulent Times 2013), p.48

[103] (Zondervan 2002), Romans 8:28, NIV

[104] (Zondervan 2002), Psalm 46:1, NIV

[105] (Zondevan 2002), 2 Corinthians 4:17-18, NIV

THE MODEST MODEL FOR HEALING & DELIVERANCE
Seven Steps of Spiritual Healing & Deliverance

Spiritual healing and deliverance are biblical promises available to every Christian believer. These promises are found in Scripture throughout both the Old Testament and New Testament, which speak to

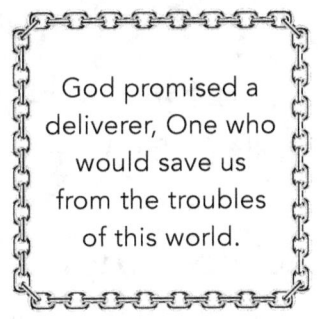

God promised a deliverer, One who would save us from the troubles of this world.

healing of spiritual, physical, and emotional conditions. God promised a deliverer, One who would save us from the troubles of this world. While these promises are available to us, there are necessary actions a person must take to receive healing and deliverance, as covered in this section.

These actions include:

Step One: Acknowledging the need for healing and deliverance

Step Two: Believing in the possibility of healing and deliverance

Step Three: Confessing sins hindering one from receiving healing and deliverance

Step Four: Determination in the pursuit of healing and deliverance

Step Five: Evaluating areas where healing and deliverance is needed

Step Six: Forgiveness of self and others to achieve healing and deliverance

Step Seven: Glorifying God, who is the One who grants spiritual healing and deliverance

Acknowledging

Until a person acknowledges the need for healing and deliverance, they will continue to suffer from past pain and trauma. The most significant sources of our suffering are the lies we tell ourselves.[106] We tell ourselves

To admit our faults and flaws is an act of submission to the One who can heal and deliver us.

that everything is fine in our life, all while suffering from physical, spiritual, and emotional generational curses, strongholds, and world troubles. We know a problem exists

---

[106] (Van Der Kolk, M.D. 2014), p. 11

in our hearts but resist acknowledging our sins[107] or trouble caused by others.

The sin of pride keeps people suffering because they are too prideful to admit the need for help. A prideful person's mind tells them that the admission of help would somehow point out their imperfections. Jesus is the only unflawed person; all others have faults and flaws. To admit our faults and flaws is an act of submission to the One who can heal and deliver us. Submission requires humility and is required by God as He resists the proud but gives grace to the humble.[108] Every day, God tests us through people, pain, or problems.[109] However, we can be healed when we humble ourselves before God and submit to His authority.

Submission is a form of acknowledging a source of legitimate authority. *"Submit yourself therefore to God. Resist the devil, and he will flee from you."*[110] Submission is the state where one has placed themselves under authority or yielded to that authority. Until we submit to God, we are powerless and have no authority to remove Satan from our lives or situations.[111] On the contrary, submitting to God gives us the power necessary to rid ourselves of the grips of the enemy,

---

[107] (Fleagle 2022 p. 76)

[108] (Zondervan 2002), 1 Peter 5:5-6, NIV

[109] (Lucado, You'll Get Through This: Hope and Help for Your Turbulent Times 2013), p. 177

[110] (Zondevan 2002), James 4:7, NIV

[111] (Harrigton and Harrington 2011), p.47

who has no power over us nor any unsettled claims against us! Seeking out help from the Lord and others is an example of submission and acknowledging the need for help.

Seeking help is a significant first step toward a healthier life. Seeking professional help from a therapist, counselor, or psychologist who specializes in abuse or other mental health illnesses can be part of the initial steps toward wellness.[112] Unfortunately, in some cultures, there are stigmas associated with seeking the help of a professional counselor. Fearing what others may think of them, people suffer in silence. The stigma derives from the perception of being looked upon as "weak" or "crazy" when they solicit the support of a therapist—quite the opposite. People who seek professional and spiritual assistance exhibit courage when they admit they are somehow flawed and need help to overcome whatever keeps them from receiving the healing and deliverance they desire. They realize they do not have to accept life as it is and can work toward lasting, authentic change.

For most people, acceptance is rarely a goal. Instead, they desire a change in circumstances that led to sorrow. Acceptance is often equated with failure—failure to succeed, improve, and transcend one's old self.[113] Failed attempts are not always readily accepted. Sometimes,

---

[112] (M. Morgan 2019), p. 33
[113] (Newberg, M.D., and Waldman 2009, p.229

...we must embrace God, who invites us to find rest and comfort in His love.

acknowledging the need for help is misinterpreted as admitting failures. Failing to get to the goal of change unconsciously keeps one in a state of accepting failed attempts. Taking no action is an action of complacency, which delays healing. One cannot expect to heal from past pain and trauma while in a state of complacency. Embracing our experiences helps achieve healing and deliverance. We must first embrace the harm of living in a fallen world where we are flawed and full of faults. Secondly, we must embrace God, who invites us to find rest and comfort in His love. Lastly, we must embrace the highs and lows of life so that we are healed and transformed by God.[114] Our transformation starts with acknowledging the need for a transformed life.

Jesus settled all debts through His blood shed on the cross for all of humanity. The blood of Jesus has miraculous power to save, set free, and redeem us from the attacks of our adversary. David's awful agony over his sin was conquered once he acknowledged it.[115] He declared in Psalm 32:1, *"Blessed is the one whose transgressions are forgiven, whose sins are not covered."* In verse five of the same

---

[114] (Allender, PhD. 1999), p.30
[115] (Fleagle 2022), p. 76

chapter, he declares, *"Then I acknowledged my sin to you and did not cover up my iniquity. I said, 'I will confess my transgressions to the LORD.' And you forgave the guilt of my sin."*[116] We must acknowledge the need for healing and

The fool is the one who refuses to believe God exists.

acknowledge the One who has the power to heal us. In these passages, we find that David acknowledged his sin, confessed his transgressions, and God forgave him.

Believing

We live in a world that is pregnant with the "there is no God" philosophy.[117] David declares in Psalm 14:1, *The fool says in his heart, "There is no God."*[118] The fool is the one who refuses to believe God exists. There is no sincere hope apart from God. Without God and His Word as our roadmap, and without the Holy Spirit as our pilot, modern people are bewildered and traveling in high gear without direction.[119]

A significant component of the Christian faith is rooted in the Word of God and a strong belief in Jesus Christ, the Son of God and our Lord and Savior. We must believe in

---

[116] (Zondevan 2002), Psalm 32:1, 5, NIV

[117] (Fleagle 2022), p.29

[118] (Zondevan 2002), Psalm 14:1, NIV

[119] (Fleagle 2022), p. 30

the promises of God. We must believe that God is not a man that He should lie.[120] God is trustworthy, while people cannot always be trusted. If God promises healing to those in need, we can trust His promise. God never reneges on His Word. If God promised to deliver us from the troubles and temptations of this world, we believe what He says. Our faith helps us believe all that God declares.

Faith is a gift from God[121] that we utilize to help us believe in healing and deliverance. Faith is an exercise in belief. When our identity rests in anything other than Christ, we will return to that old identity as a reference point for how to do life.[122] As we become new creatures in Christ, the old is passed away.[123] Furthermore, as we become new creatures in Christ, we become more like Christ and can believe that Jesus is who He says He is: the world's Savior. We can believe He did what the Bible says He did. He died for the world's sins.[124] Believing in Jesus Christ as the world's Savior gives us hope for today and for our future. We can also trust and believe if God healed and delivered us in the past, He can do it again. As believers in

---

[120] (Zondevan 2002), Numbers 23:19, NIV

[121] (Zondervan 2002), Ephesians 2:8-9, NIV

[122] (Vanderbush and Eaton, 2020), p.75

[123] (Zondevan 2002), 2 Corinthians 5:17, NIV

[124] (Lucado, God Will Use This for Good: Surviving the Mess of Life 2013), p.34

Christ, we understand God is not a respecter of persons;[125] He can heal and deliver anyone.

As part of becoming a new creation, we learn to transform our minds from our old ways of thinking.[126] The first lesson in the renewal of the mind is not to believe old carnal feelings and thoughts when they come back after prayers for healing.[127] Furthermore, what one feels or thinks matters once we believe it and give it life and power.[128] Having a solid conviction in the power of Christ and what He says about healing and deliverance brings healing and deliverance in one's life.

Mind-body medicine uses the power of thoughts and emotions to influence physical health. It has become so widely accepted today that it is difficult to recall when it was considered fantasy.[129] People with a strong belief in their minds will begin to feel and experience what they perceive. For instance, a woman who strongly believes in her mind that she is pregnant may begin to experience pregnancy symptoms, such as nausea and weight gain. From a spiritual perspective, if a person believes they are healed from physical infirmities, they may no longer experience

---

[125] (Zondervan 2002), Romans 2:11, NIV
[126] (Zondervan 2002), Romans 1:2, NIV
[127] (Sanford and Sanford 1991), p.29
[128] (Sanford and Sanford 1991), p.29
[129] (Bradley Hagerty 2009), p. 48

symptoms of illness. People who believe God can heal them can experience better days because of their faith in Jesus.

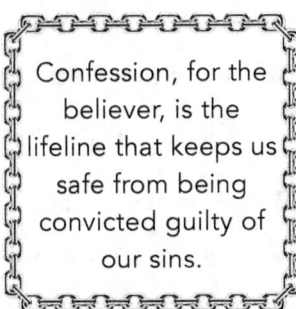

Confession, for the believer, is the lifeline that keeps us safe from being convicted guilty of our sins.

Confession

Confession is a necessary step in acknowledging the need for a Savior. Additionally, confession is the acknowledgment of guilt, which is required to receive a pardon or the forgiveness of sin. When we confess our sins and our need for a savior, we hold ourselves accountable to God, who is fully aware of our sinful nature. Confession grants us the hope of receiving forgiveness. God is faithful and will forgive our sins and purify us from all unrighteousness[130] when we confess our sins.

Confession, for the believer, is the lifeline that keeps us safe from being convicted guilty of our sins. It is both therapeutic and soothing for the soul. It frees us from guilt and shame of our wrongdoing. Confession is an arrow in the Christian's arsenal[131] that destroys sin. Confession is not a long, drawn-out process; instead, it is simply admitting the wrongdoing and admitting that we are sinners in need of a Savior.[132] It is that simple. The more challenging aspect of

---

[130] (Zondervan 2002), 1 John 1:9, NIV

[131] (Fleagle 2022), p. 76

[132] (Lucado, God Will Use This for Good: Surviving the Mess of Life 2013), p.33

confession is repentance, which requires a change of heart and behavior. We must "repent, then, and turn to God so that sins may be wiped away."[133]

Repentance means coming to sufficient hatred of our sins and sinful nature that when we reckon them as dead, death happens because we do not want them any longer.[134] We must loathe our sin so much that we

> God created us with the capacity to recover quickly from difficulties, including physical and mental trauma.

are willing to turn away from it completely. To repent is to be sorry for the hurt we have caused the Lord and others by what has lodged in our hearts and what we have done; it is being willing to die for what we have been and allowing God to change us into what He wants us to be.[135] Like confession, repentance is another powerful tool in spiritual warfare.[136] As we put our trust in God to fight our battles. We can trust that confession is cleansing the soul. It allows God to wipe away the stains and debris that cause sin.

---

[133] (Zondevan 2002), Acts 3:19, NIV

[134] (Sandford and Sandford, A Comprehensive Guide to Deliverance and Inner Healing 1998), p.61

[135] (Sandford and Sandford, A Comprehensive Guide to Deliverance and Inner Healing 1998), p.60

[136] (Sandford and Sandford, A Comprehensive Guide to Deliverance and Inner Healing 1998), p.41

Determination

As human beings, we belong to a highly resilient species. Since time immemorial, we have rebounded from our relentless wars, countless disasters (both natural and manufactured), and the violence and betrayal in our own lives.[137] God created us with the capacity to recover quickly from difficulties, including physical and mental trauma. We have determination and resilience working hand in hand. Resilience enables us to bounce back from adversity, and determination keeps us heading in the right direction. We must be determined to live for Christ, regardless of the trouble that comes our way. Our resilience is what enables us to live for Christ.

Having determination requires a mindset change. This change is developed from daily practice and is necessary to overcome past hurt and trauma. Renewing the spirit of our minds[138] is about learning to hear the voice of God by allowing time for the spirit to build a friendship with the Holy Spirit and bond spirit to spirit.[139] Hearing from God allows us to heal and be delivered from past trauma. Moreover, hearing from God builds determination to be strong, courageous, and fearless because we know God is with us and for us.

---

[137] (Van Der Kolk, M.D. 2014), Prologue
[138] (Zondervan 2002), Romans 12:2, NIV
[139] (Vallotton 2020), p. 43

Tragically enough, so many Christians have never learned the simple lesson of the continuous battle to subdue their minds and feelings.[140] Our thoughts have the power to create actions. When we think about the wrong things, we can expect sinful behavior. The Apostle Paul says to think about whatever is "true, noble, right, and pure and whatever is admirable, excellent, and praiseworthy."[141] Thinking about such things requires determination and discipline. The discipline every born-anew Christian must learn is how to recognize when he is resurrecting an old fallen practice to haul it restfully back to the cross again.[142] To be disciplined is to be determined.

Evaluation

Traumatic experiences leave traces, whether on a large scale (on our histories and cultures) or close to home, on our families, with dark secrets imperceptibly passed down through generations.[143] They also leave traces on our minds, emotions, capacity for joy and intimacy, and biology and immune systems.[144] To receive spiritual healing and deliverance, the areas where healing is necessary must be evaluated. One may require spiritual, emotional, or physical

---

[140] (Van Der Kolk, M.D. 2014), p. 40

[141] (Zondevan 2002), Philippians 4:8, NIV

[142] (Sanford and Sanford 1991), p.31

[143] (Van Der Kolk, M.D. 2014), Prologue

[144] (Van Der Kolk, M.D. 2014), Prologue

healing and deliverance from generational curses, strongholds, or trouble. There may be multiple combinations of the areas listed where healing and deliverance are necessary. Trauma may be multi-level and deeply rooted across vast areas of life and in response to life's vicissitudes spanning various timespans.

> When we ask God to show us ourselves, we can expect Him to do so.

A large population of people suffer from adverse childhood experiences carried over into adulthood and desire healing and deliverance from those experiences. Soul-searching is an excellent place to determine where to begin with healing and deliverance. Experiencing feelings of hurt and disappointment, anger, rage, anxiety, and depression may point to specific areas where healing is necessary. Often, a person may not know precisely what is causing them distress. They need the assistance of a professional therapist or spiritual advisor to help them identify the areas plaguing them.

Self-examination should occur regularly to see if any offensive ways[145] must be dealt with, which may be the cause of the brokenness. When we ask God to show us ourselves, we can expect Him to do so. This request of God can be exciting and frightening at the same time. It is

---

[145] (Zondervan 2002), Psalm 139:23-24, NIV

Forgiveness is the willingness to let go of the hurtful past.

exciting to know that when we talk to God, He hears us and will respond. It is frightening because there may be areas in which we may need to change—and change can be difficult. During self-examination, we may discover that we are harboring "bitterness, rage, and anger, brawling, and slander."[146] Harboring such feelings only delays healing. Consequently, understanding the triggers surrounding these unwanted feelings helps facilitate the healing process.

Perhaps God will show us, during the evaluation process, that we need to change how we communicate with others and not let any unwholesome talk come out of our mouths, but only what helps build up others according to their needs.[147] Once God shows us the error of our ways, we are to do better to become better. Having an evaluation plan would be an excellent place to start when setting out on the journey to becoming whole. An evaluation plan helps us turn information into implementation, thereby receiving the desired healing and deliverance.

---

[146] (Zondevan 2002), Ephesian 4:31, NIV
[147] (Zondevan 2002), Ephesian 4:29, NIV

Forgiveness

Forgiveness is a topic of vulnerability when dealing with the transgressions of others. In relationships, such as in a marriage or other intimate relationships, forgiveness of offenses is necessary to have a healthy relationship. Forgiveness is the willingness to let go of the hurtful past. It is the decision to suffer no longer, to heal the heart and soul.[148] The act of forgiving is not necessarily letting someone off the hook for offenses committed but acknowledging that we are not perfect and need forgiveness of our sins toward God and others.

Forgiveness is the prerequisite for lasting healing.[149] We cannot always start by forgiving from our heart, but we can begin by deciding to forgive.[150] To forgive from the heart means to heal emotionally. While emotions may be complicated to heal immediately, we can decide to forgive immediately. Forgiveness frees the heart to heal and releases the burden of unforgiveness.

It can be challenging to release a person from the burden of sins committed toward us when hurting. It is also challenging to love the unlovable. However, God loved us while we were sinners,[151] and He still does. Forgiveness is a

---

[148] (Jampolsky, M.D. 1999), p.17

[149] (Kylstra and Kylstra 2005), p. 33

[150] (Kylstra and Kylstra 2005), p. 39

[151] (Zondervan 2002), Romans 5:8, NIV

gift from God. We receive the gift of forgiveness through our faith in Jesus Christ. There is nothing we can do to earn this gift other than believe in the Lordship of Jesus.

It is through our faith that we repent and receive forgiveness. Repentance and forgiveness address the root of unforgiveness, and we can receive inner healing. When this happens, the demonic carefully constructed theatre of operations is demolished and must leave.[152] When the roots of unforgiveness are destroyed, we can receive healing, and unforgiveness can no longer create chaos. Forgiveness becomes a lifestyle that allows us to ask God for the forgiveness of our sins and allows us to forgive others.

God's Word spells out His requirement for Christians: We are to relate to one another without bitterness, grudges, or anything that puts up a barrier between us and our brother or sister in Christ. No matter what the offense, He says, "Forgive."[153] Christians are to forgive others, just as Christ has forgiven us.[154] As freely as we want forgiveness, we should forgive others. During a grave offense, Jesus prayed for those who were harming Him. It is nearly impossible to imagine forgiveness of that magnitude. The forgiveness at Calvary is nothing comparable to any violation we may

---

[152] (Sandford and Sandford, A Comprehensive Guide to Deliverance and Inner Healing 1998), p.29

[153] (Kylstra and Kylstra 2005), p. 37

[154] (Zondervan 2002), Ephesians 4:32, NIV

encounter. There is no sin or greater offense than the crucifixion of Christ. Nevertheless, amid execution, Jesus prayed for forgiveness. Imagine a person while beaten, robbed, raped, molested, or worst and praying for those committing the crime. Jesus did. If He did, so should we.

> ...God can forgive us of our sins and remove our transgressions from us as far as the east is from the west...

Not only should we ask for forgiveness from God and forgive others, but we should also forgive ourselves. Individuals suffer from self-damnation due to past mistakes and bad decisions, causing them to become remorseful. Guilt and shame haunt them daily. Forgiving ourselves comes from our understanding of how God forgives us. Hebrews 10:22 states, *"Let us draw near to God with a sincere heart and with the full assurance that faith brings, having our hearts sprinkled to cleanse us from a guilty conscience and having our bodies washed with pure water."* Seeing that God can forgive us of our sins and remove our transgressions from us as far as the east is from the west,[155] we, too, should forgive ourselves to experience healing and deliverance from sin.

Forgiveness is the most potent medicine for healing thoughts that cause extensive symptoms. Forgiveness is a

---

[155] (Zondervan 2002), Psalm 103:12, NIV

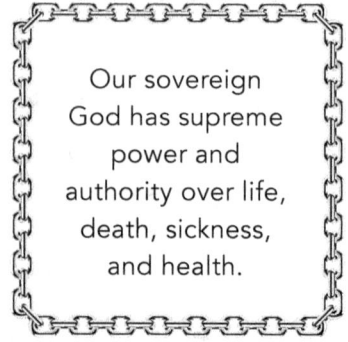

Our sovereign God has supreme power and authority over life, death, sickness, and health.

powerful, unique, and miraculous healer capable of making all these symptoms disappear.[156] Forgiveness has the power to cure anger, bitterness, depression, stress, and isolation, among other symptoms. God gives only the best gifts, and forgiveness is one of the greatest!

God

God is the conduit by which we receive healing and deliverance. Our sovereign God has supreme power and authority over life, death, sickness, and health. God has power over demonic forces we encounter through generational curses, strongholds, and trouble. God, Jehovah Rapha, is a healer by His very nature and name.[157] He wants everything to go well with us, and we will be healthy.[158] God is the One who *"forgives all our iniquities, heals our diseases, redeems us from the pit, and crowns us with steadfast love and mercy."*[159] It is through the blood of Christ that we are

---

156 (Jampolsky, M.D. 1999), p. 31
157 (Zondervan 1989), Exodus 15:26, NRSV
158 (Zondervan 1989), 3 John 3:1-2, NRSV
159 (Zondervan 1989), Psalm 103:2-4, NRSV

redeemed and receive forgiveness of sins.[160] Our redemption affords us the precious gift of healing and deliverance.

Redemption means buying back or recovering by paying a price.[161] Spiritual redemption can be found only in Christ, God's one and only son,[162] who provided the ransom to free us from our captivity to sin.[163] Jesus paid the price with His shed blood, freeing us from sin and sickness.[164] Redemption through Christ is the central theme of a Christian's spiritual life, delivering us from the curse of eternal death and freeing us to live an abundant life in Christ.[165] God continually redeems people from poverty, isolation, loneliness, emptiness, depression, alienation, and sin.[166]

God is the only One who can redeem people, but people are often used as God's agents. Humankind partners with God to help free others through words of encouragement, acts of kindness, or by lending a helping hand through acts of service. Jesus declares that when we feed the hungry, clothe the needy, or visit the sick and shut in[167], we become a vessel He uses to help deliver someone from their many troubles. Surely, God can do this on His own, but our

---

[160] (Zondervan 2002), Ephesians 1:7, NIV

[161] (McMinn, Ph.D 2011), p. 291

[162] (Zondervan 2002), John 3:16, NIV

[163] (McMinn, Ph.D 2011), p. 302

[164] (Zondevan 2002), Colossians 1:14, NIV

[165] (McMinn, Ph.D 2011), p. 298

[166] (McMinn, Ph.D 2011), p. 298

[167] (Zondervan 2002), Matthew 25:27-40, NIV

Christian discipline of serving allows us to collaborate and cooperate with God to accomplish His will on earth in the lives of His people. Through collaboration and cooperation, God distributes grace, mercy, healing, and deliverance to those in need. God not only redeems us spiritually but also delivers us from many perils and hardships, often through the kindness of others. People partner with God to help free others through words of encouragement, acts of kindness, or by lending a helping hand through acts of service.

God bestows grace, mercy, and tender loving kindness toward us daily; even when we lament our troubles, His mercies never end.[168] God initiates grace by giving it freely as a gift through the death and resurrection of Jesus Christ.[169] We must get to know Him personally to understand God's character and graciousness toward us genuinely. We do this by reading the Word of God, praying to God, and worshipping Him.

The phrase *sola scriptura* is from the Latin *sola*, having the idea of "alone," "ground," and "base," and the Word *scriptura* means "writings" referring to the Scriptures. *Sola scriptura* means Scripture alone is authoritative for the faith and practice of the Christian.[170] When we read the Word of God, we can trust that the Bible is complete, authoritative,

---

[168] (Zondevan 2002), Lamentations 3:22-23, NIV

[169] (Vanderbush and Eaton 2020), p.82

[170] (Settecase 2022), Is Sola Scriptura Biblical, August 20, 2022

and accurate. According to 2 Timothy 3:16, *"All Scripture is God-breathed and is useful for teaching, rebuking, correcting and training in righteousness."*[171] Reading the Word allows us to learn the character of God and understand His dominion over everything. There is nothing God cannot do. There is no place we can go where God is not present. Wherever we are, God is there. When we are doing well, God is there. When we are deep in the slums of life, God is also there. Because He is where we are, we can believe He watches over us and cares for us. What may seem impossible to us is possible with God! No matter where we find ourselves, we always have access to God through prayer.

> Prayer is our way of communicating with God; it allows us to talk with Him.

Prayer is our way of communicating with God; it allows us to talk with Him. Fancy words are unnecessary when talking to Him because He is our heavenly Father and already knows what we need.[172] We should pray for thanksgiving, confession, special requests, and worship when praying to God. Regardless of our suffering, we can always find something to be thankful for because our situations could always be worse. We should go before the

---

[171] (Zondevan 2002), 2 Timothy 3:16, NIV
[172] (Zondervan 1989), Matthew 6:8, NRSV

Lord with thanksgiving because He is the One who can make our lives better. When praying to God, believers must confess their sins and acknowledge that we need a savior.

After we confess our sins, we can go to God and make our requests known to Him, *"and the peace of God will guard our hearts and minds during troubled times."*[173] Trusting entirely in God allows us to worship Him even before the battle ends.[174] We can worship God amid being anxious, depressed, financially destitute, and sick. During difficult seasons of bereavement, we must worship God, knowing that *"blessed are those who mourn, for they will be comforted."*[175] The Holy Spirit comforts us. But we, too, can find comfort and encouragement in others. God will send angels here on earth to help us through turbulent times.

> The healing provided by God is nothing new, as many received healing in ancient times.

The healing provided by God is nothing new, as many received healing in ancient times. Countless stories are recorded in the Bible of people healed from spiritual, emotional, and physical disabilities such as blindness, congenital disabilities, diseases, generational curses,

---

[173] (Zondervan 2002), Ephesians 4:6-7, NIV
[174] (Zondervan 2002), 2 Chronicles 20:15, NIV
[175] (Zondevan 2002), Matthew 5:4, NIV

strongholds, and everyday troubles. These stories prove He can do what He has done before. He is the same God, yesterday, today, and always.[176] He does not change. God can perform the same healing and deliverance He did for biblical characters King David, Job, the blind, the woman with the issue of blood, and countless others.

King David understood the importance of spiritual inner healing. He commanded his soul to bless the Lord so that he would not forget the benefits of God. Those benefits included forgiveness of sin and healing of diseases.[177] David points out that God is compassionate and gracious, slow to anger, and abounding in love. So even when times are difficult, he could find healing for his soul through blessing the Lord almighty.

Job suffered more than anyone in the Bible. He lost it all. It's the classic story of riches to rags and back to riches! He suffered spiritually, emotionally, and physically. Job had at least three terrible friends who were jealous of his wealth and blamed him for all that had happened to him. They gave him evil counsel. Job was misunderstood in his social circumstances—like most are today. Even though God was silent during Job's suffering, God was also present. Job's suffering was no surprise to God. Never once did Job file

---

[176] (Zondervan 2002), Hebrews 13:8, NIV
[177] (Zondervan 1989), Psalm 103, NIV

any complaints against God. Job teaches us valuable life lessons that we can apply whenever we find ourselves in spiritual, emotional, and physical calamity. We can take heart in knowing that whatever we may be going through, while it may catch us off guard, God is on the case.

When we lose our jobs, find ourselves in a nasty divorce, or experience the death of loved ones that shake us to our core, God is not surprised. He is ready to restore us to even better conditions,[178] just as He did for Job. Restoration may not look like we want or expect, but God's plan for our life is better than anything we can imagine, and we must trust in His sovereignty. Job remained faithful to God. As a result, *poor* Job became *blessed* Job. Like Job, we can go from "Woe is me!" to "Wow! I am free!"

Jesus often healed people from blindness, the earliest being recorded in the Gospel of Mark, dealing with a blind man in Bethsaida.[179] When Jesus arrived in Bethsaida, the people begged Him to touch the blind man. He obliged their request most unusually. After leading the man away from the village, He placed saliva on the man's eyes and asked, "Can you see anything?"[180] Jesus repeated the process one other time before the man could see clearly.

---

[178] (Zondervan 1989), Job 42:10 NRSV
[179] (Zondevan 2002), Mark 8:22-26, NIV
[180] (Zondervan 2002), Mark 8:23, NIV

Lessons Learned from This Scenario:

✓   When we ask Jesus to heal us, He complies.

✓   We can lead others to Jesus for healing. The text says that "the people" brought the blind man to him.

✓   We see that Jesus may lead us to a place of isolation, away from onlookers, to perform healing.

✓   We also see that Jesus employed a very unusual healing method by placing saliva on the man's eyes. God still uses unorthodox methods for our healing today.

✓   Although the two-step process was intentional on Jesus' behalf, healing may take time and require repeated applications of the required remedy.

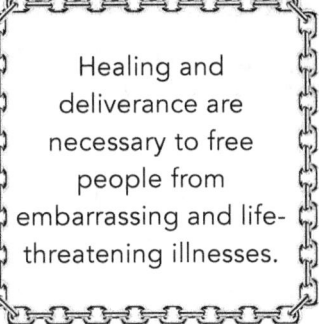

Healing and deliverance are necessary to free people from embarrassing and life-threatening illnesses.

Another account of biblical healing, found in Mark 5, tells a story about an unnamed woman with an issue of blood.[181] She suffered from an illness for twelve long years and was not finding any relief from regular doctor's visits. She spent all she had and was not any better. Individuals suffer from physical ailments for years sometimes. Rather than getting better, their condition

---

[181] (Zondervan 1989), Mark 5:25-34, NRSV

worsens often, and they become immune to the medications. One can only imagine how embarrassing this illness was for this woman. Healing and deliverance are necessary to free people from embarrassing and life-threatening illnesses.

How long could this poor woman live like this? Not long, for sure. Consider how she may have been depressed, lonely, and desperate. People around her had to know something was ailing her, but no one could help her, not even if they wanted to. People in her community were forbidden to touch her because she was ceremonially unclean and hemorrhaging. Only One person could help her, and she

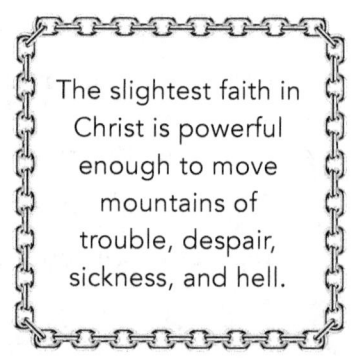

The slightest faith in Christ is powerful enough to move mountains of trouble, despair, sickness, and hell.

heard He was coming to town. Her chance for healing was in view. Her faith prompted her to do something different. She pressed her way to reach out to Jesus for healing. She acknowledged that she was gravely ill and needed help.

She believed that Jesus could heal her and was determined to touch Him. This woman was so determined that she pressed her way to get to Him no matter how large the crowd. In response to her faith, Jesus told her, "Daughter, your faith has healed you. Go in peace and be freed from your suffering."[182] If only we could have this magnitude of faith when faced with physical illnesses, we, too, can be healed! The slightest faith in Christ is powerful enough to move mountains[183] of trouble, despair, sickness, and hell.

The Apostle Paul had a change of heart and mind following his road to Damascus experience. Paul had wrong attitudes, thinking patterns, ideas, and desires. That is, until he had a face-to-face encounter with God. Paul experienced a dramatic transformation and is known for writing most of the New Testament.

Paul was known as Saul before his conversion. He intensely persecuted the followers of Jesus. Paul later encouraged the Church of Corinth that *"the weapons we fight with are not the weapons of the world. On the contrary, they have the divine power to demolish strongholds. 5 We demolish arguments and every pretension that sets itself up against the knowledge of God, and we take captive every thought to make it obedient to Christ."*[184] He understood what it meant to demolish strongholds because he had suffered from them until he was healed and delivered on the road to Damascus. He became an all-important ambassador for Christ to help others become free from a life of trouble and suffering.

---

[182] (Zondevan 2002), Mark 5:34, NIV

[183] (Zondervan 2002), Matthew 17:20-21, NIV

[184] (Zondevan 2002), 2 Corinthians 10:4-5, NIV

God can use the trouble in our lives to accomplish His perfect plan. Consider how He did this for Joseph, who went from the pit to the palace as part of God's plan. Although Joseph experienced sibling rivalry, was sold into slavery and was accused of a crime that he did not commit, he found favor with God every step of the way. Joseph experienced the same troubles back then that we are faced with today. In the end, Joseph realized what others intended to harm him, God intended it for good, to preserve people's lives, as he does today.[185] Joseph understood that the trouble he experienced was not only for him to live and be well, but to save others.

God also uses our troubles to draw us closer to Him. True healing and deliverance occur when we consider our *"various trials as joy, knowing that testing our faith produces endurance."*[186] If we allow it, our troubles can draw us closer to God, where we should desire to be. God wants to be close to us and, therefore, will allow troubles to come our way. Whenever we are in trouble, rather than having a pity party, we can have a praise party because God is with us and can deliver us from the hands of the enemy.

---

[185] (Zondervan 1989), Genesis 50:20, NRSV
[186] (Zondervan 1989), James 1:2, NRSV

APPLYING THE 7-STEP MODEL TO ACHIEVE HEALING & DELIVERANCE

While healing and deliverance are no easy feats, the following model will help one achieve spiritual healing and deliverance. *The Modest Model for Healing and Deliverance* contains seven steps to facilitate healing and deliverance. The model may be helpful as a starting point for anyone who may not know how to start their journey to healing.

The **first** step in the model is *Acknowledgement*. One must acknowledge that something in life is a mess and must change. Acknowledgment is the realization that something is out of place in life and needs addressing. Denial is the enemy of progress. The longer a person denies and does not acknowledge it, the further they get from being healed. One should start by acknowledging that they are a sinner who needs saving. They should acknowledge that they need someone more powerful in their life who can see them through their troubled lives. No one is more powerful than God!

Application:

Pause to *"Acknowledge"* the need for healing and deliverance in your life. Acknowledge past and/or present trauma requiring healing and deliverance in your life.

Meditation Scripture:

"Search me, O God, and know my heart; test me and know my anxious thoughts. See if there is any offensive way in me and lead me in the way everlasting."
–PSALM 139:23-24, NIV

Prayer:

Dear Heavenly Father,

I come to you *"acknowledging"* the need for healing and deliverance. Apart from you, I cannot do anything, but I can do all things with you. I acknowledge that while my life is not perfect, I am perfectly forgiven and loved by you.

Notes:

_____

_____

_____

_____

The **second** step is to *Believe*. By this, one must have an unwavering belief that God is who He says He is and desires His children to be whole. One must believe what the Word of God says about who He is and what He can do. He can do immeasurably more than all we ask or imagine, according to His power that is at work within us.[187] We must believe that God can heal and deliver us from any miserable life situation or circumstance.

Application:
Pause to "*Believe*" that God is who He says He is, and that He desires to see you healed and delivered.

Meditation Scripture:
"But I will restore you to health and heal your wounds,"
declares the LORD."
–JEREMIAH 30:17, NIV

Prayer:
Dear Heavenly Father,

I come to you "*believing*" all that your Word says about me. I believe that your son, Jesus Christ, died for my sins. I believe that your promises concerning me are true. I believe you can heal and deliver me from all sicknesses and diseases.

---

[187] (Zondevan 2002), Ephesians 3:20, NIV

Notes:

_____

_____

_____

_____

The **third** step is *Confession*. Individuals should confess their sins to God. One must confess the need and dependence on God. There is no amount of sin that confession cannot cover. God loves us so much that He will forgive those who confess their sins. We may hide from others, but we cannot hide from God. Confessing what He already knows is essential to releasing guilt and receiving healing and deliverance.

Application:

Pause to "*Confess*" that you are a sinner in need of a savior who can heal and deliver you. Confess your sinful ways and lifestyle. Confess your need for a renewed mindset.

Meditation Scripture:

"If you declare with your mouth, "Jesus is Lord," and believe in your heart that God raised him from the dead, you will be saved. For it is with your heart that you believe and are justified, and it is with your mouth that you profess your faith and are saved."
–ROMANS 10:9-10, NIV

Prayer:

Dear Heavenly Father,

I *"confess"* that I am a sinner in need of a savior. I pray that you will create in me a clean heart and that I might turn from my wicked ways. Lord, allow my humble confession to heal and deliver me from all past and/or present trauma.

Notes:

_____

_____

_____

_____

The **fourth** step in the process is *Determination*. After acknowledging the need for healing, a person should believe in their heart that God can heal and deliver them. After confessing their specific sins to God, they become determined to get healed, doing whatever it takes to obtain it, which may mean having someone hold them accountable, or by giving up something or someone they love. Healing and deliverance may come with a sacrifice, and they must be willing to pay the price.

Application:

Pause to renew your mind to have the *"Determination"* needed to achieve healing and deliverance. Clear your mind from any distractions that would cause you to lose focus on your goal of becoming healed and delivered from past and/or present trauma.

Meditation Scripture:

"Do not conform to the pattern of this world but be transformed by the renewing of your mind. Then you will be able to test and approve what God's will is—his good, pleasing, and perfect will."
–ROMANS 12:2, NIV

Prayer:

Dear Heavenly Father,

Allow your Holy Spirit to strengthen my *"determination"* to pursue healing and deliverance. While I understand that reliving trauma may be difficult, lead and guide me as I set out to receive the promise of healing and deliverance.

Notes:

_____

_____

_____

_____

The **fifth** step is the *Evaluation* process. Consider where there is the most suffering to begin the evaluation process. Is a wounded soul that comes from word curses spoken over their life? Maybe it is a broken spirit from being abused, mistreated, abandoned, or neglected. Are generational curses stifling spiritual growth and maturity? Take a closer look through the evaluation process to determine what areas require improvement and start there.

Application:

Pause to *"Evaluate"* the areas in which you may require healing and deliverance.

Meditation Scripture:

"Examine yourselves to see whether you are in the faith; test yourselves. Do you not realize that Christ Jesus is in you— unless, of course, you fail the test?"

–2 CORINTHIANS 13:5, NIV

Prayer:

Dear Heavenly Father,

Help me to *"evaluate"* past and/or present trauma that may be hindering me from being the person who you created me to be. Allow your Holy Spirit to speak to me and show me where I might have suppressed any hurtful memories so that I can heal from past hurt.

Notes:

_____

_____

_____

_____

Forgiveness is the **sixth** step in *The Modest Model for Healing and Deliverance*. Unforgiveness is an awful sin that keeps us from becoming healed. Ask God for forgiveness, forgive others, and most importantly, forgive oneself. Vow to release unforgiveness that makes one spiritually, emotionally, and physically ill. Use Jesus as the model of forgiveness. Pray and ask God to forgive those offended. Then, forgive others just as you would want forgiveness from God.

Application:

Pause to "*Forgive*" others and yourself for past and/or present offenses. Ask God to forgive you for your offenses against Him and others.

Meditation Scripture:

"Get rid of all bitterness, rage, and anger, brawling and slander, along with every form of malice. Be kind and compassionate to one another, forgiving each other, just as in Christ God forgave you."
–EPHESIANS 4:31-32, NIV

Prayer:

Dear Heavenly Father,

I am coming to you to ask for your forgiveness. Lord, I "*forgive*" those who have trespassed against me. I release all unforgiveness that may be preventing me from receiving healing and deliverance in my life.

Notes:

_____

_____

_____

_____

Finally, the **seventh** step in the process, and the most important, is *God*. If one remembers nothing else in life, remember that God is the One who cares enough about you to see you healed and delivered. Remember that He may allow trouble to come into life to draw people closer to Him. God is so unique that human words cannot fathom how remarkable He is. While much can be written about God, describing His nature, character, and blessings would never be enough. Rather than attempting to explain God, we should exclaim His goodness! *"Let the redeemed of the Lord say so!"*[188]

Application:

Pause to glorify "GOD," who is the giver of deliverance! (G.O.D.)

---

[188] (Zondevan 2002), Psalm 107:2, NIV

Meditation Scripture:

"Declare his glory among the nations, his marvelous deeds among all peoples."

–1 CHRONICLES 16:24, NIV

Prayer:

Dear Heavenly Father,

Thank you for being "GOD," my heavenly Father who promises to never leave nor forsake me. God, I glorify you with my life!

Notes:

_____

_____

_____

_____

―――――――――――――――――――――

If there were an eighth step of the model, it would be to repeat steps one through seven. There will always be something in life that causes discomfort. Applying *The Modest Model for Healing and Deliverance* is relevant to every situation in life to obtain spiritual healing and deliverance.

Whether trauma of the mind, body, or soul, and no matter how minor or significant the circumstances may be, a person should always start with acknowledging the need for healing, believing in the power of healing, confessing the need for it, and confessing belief in the One who heals. One must remain determined to achieve healing, perform continuous evaluation of the areas in which healing and deliverance are needed, forgive others and self, and finally, ask God for healing and deliverance. He is the One who heals and delivers! For God, nothing is impossible!

MANIFESTATION OF HEALING

After close examination of the topics of spiritual healing and deliverance in this work, let's return to the questions presented at the very beginning. What is spiritual healing and deliverance? If there is such a thing, how can one achieve it? Furthermore, if there is such a thing as spiritual healing and deliverance, what are the steps involved to achieve and maintain healing?

After a close look at not only what Scripture has to say but also what other authors have written, one can conclude that spiritual healing involves:

- inner healing of the soul

- emotional healing at the place where the mind and the body meet and

- physical healing for the body to move beyond the effects of hurt

Such effects may cause feelings of worthlessness, brokenness, and hopelessness caused by spiritual trauma.

Emotional healing involves healing maladaptive emotions of anxiety, fear, anger, and guilt. Healing emotional wounds helps to facilitate physical healing. While the scars of physical abuse may heal within

God created the spirit of man and can repair it once damaged.

a fleeting period, the fallout of physical abuse could cause long-lasting emotional dysregulation.

As spiritual healing deals with the spirit of an individual, the power of the Holy Spirit becomes necessary in the battle. One does not achieve spiritual healing apart from the One who created our spirit. God created the spirit of man and can repair it once damaged. God uses trouble and trauma to draw us closer to Him.

Deliverance is the process of liberating one from generational curses, strongholds, and trouble. People have experienced the same curses that their ancestors dealt with for generations. God promises blessings and curses for all generations. God addresses generational blessings and curses in the book of Deuteronomy. He controls life and prosperity, death, and destruction.[189] The choice is ours to choose life so that our children will live.[190] God lays out the

---

[189] (Zondervan 2002), Deuteronomy 30:15, NIV
[190] (Zondevan 2002), Deuteronomy 30:19, NIV

options and gives us the answer: choose life! Life with Christ is our best defense against generational curses!

He gives us the option to choose life with Him, Jesus, and the Holy Spirit. When we choose to live for Christ, we become a new creature, and the old has passed away. While the old has passed away, we must diligently work to renew our minds and cast down strongholds.

Casting down strongholds and imaginations helps us navigate the turbulent waters of life, if not avoid everyday troubles in life. To live for Christ does not guarantee a carefree, trouble-free life. Does God guarantee the absence of struggle and the abundance of strength? Not in this life. However, He does pledge to reconstruct our pain for a higher purpose.[191] His pledge to do so comes with a guarantee sealed by the qualities of God.

The qualities of God are the unchanging aspects of His character; they are also promises we can rely on during change.[192] God is all-knowing, sovereign, holy, merciful, and good. Moreover, because of these characteristics, we can expect to be healed and delivered from anything that does not align with His will for our lives, but we must first surrender our will to His will.

---

[191] (Lucado, God Will Use This for Good: Surviving the Mess of Life 2013), p. 20
[192] (Lucado, You'll Get Through This: Hope and Help for Your Turbulent Times 2013), p. 171

When we surrender painful memories to Christ for healing, we allow Christ to change us.[193] After we surrender the unpleasant memories of life, God can redeem us and deliver us from the painful trauma memories. God often works through people while God is redeeming us.[194] Counselors are the Lord's servants through whom He can reveal what is hidden and extend His mercy to stop, by way of the cross, our reaping of childhood sins.[195]

Christian counselors help their clients understand God by demonstrating redemption. This is not to say we teach redemption as a professor teaches a class or a pastor teaches a congregation. However, we live out a redemptive relationship in the counseling office.[196] To live out a redemptive relationship in the counseling office is to demonstrate beliefs, values, and assumptions that align with the Christian lifestyle.

A redemptive worldview in counseling is defined as a set of beliefs, values, and assumptions that cause us not only to reflect humbly and gratefully on how God is drawing us out of our captivity to sin but also to motivate us to help restore others to hope and wholeness.[197] As counselors, we

---

[193] (Linn and Linn, Healing of Memories: Transforming Past Hurts into Gifts 1984), p. 76
[194] (McMinn, Ph.D 2011), p. 299
[195] (Sandford and Sandford, A Comprehensive Guide to Deliverance and Inner Healing 1998), p. 58
[196] (McMinn, Ph.D 2011), p. 294
[197] (McMinn, Ph.D 2011), p. 291

acknowledge that we, too, can sin. We need healing, so we help others achieve the healing and deliverance that we

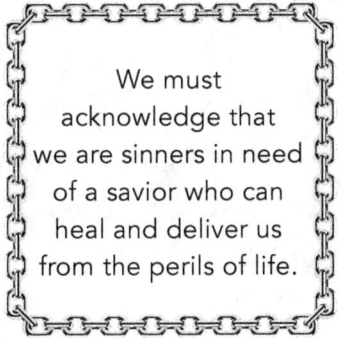

We must acknowledge that we are sinners in need of a savior who can heal and deliver us from the perils of life.

have had the opportunity to experience. We share the joy and love of Christ with those in need. Counselors help people become experts in their own lives. We empower them to take the necessary steps to secure their healing and deliverance. Among others, the steps to receive healing and deliverance include acknowledging the need, believing in it, confession, determination, evaluation, forgiveness, and finally, God who grants healing and deliverance.

As outlined in *The Modest Model Healing and Deliverance*, the first step to receiving healing and deliverance is acknowledging what our hearts tell us. We must acknowledge that we are sinners in need of a savior who can heal and deliver us from the perils of life. Let us not be like the foolish who refuse to believe that God even exists. Instead, we should put our hope and trust in the One who can heal and deliver us from sin and sickness. The life of David teaches us valuable lessons from which we can glean. While he was a great sinner, he was also a great confessor.[198]

---

[198] (Fleagle 2022), p. 77

When we remain resilient and determined, we, too, can press our way to Jesus, touch the hem of His garment, and be made whole. We must actively and consistently make an evaluation of the areas in which we need healing and deliverance, as it is not a one-time occurrence. As sinners with sinful natures, we will forever need forgiveness of our sins. We need the power of the Holy Spirit to help us because forgiveness comes, not through willpower, but through Spirit power.[199]

No one is perfect. Everyone needs forgiveness. God is the One who grants forgiveness of sin.

No one is perfect. Everyone needs forgiveness. God is the One who grants forgiveness of sin. God is the same God today as He was during biblical times. God is still in the healing and deliverance business today, just as He healed and delivered others in the Bible. He is active in the lives of His people today. Testimonies show how He continuously saves, sets free, and delivers people from the grips of the bondage of sin.

Testimonies from people like Wess Morgan, a man named Eric (last name unknown), and a woman who, for now, we will call "Redeemed", support the achievable claim of healing and deliverance even today. These people are

---

[199] (Linn and Linn, Healing of Memories: Transforming Past Hurts into Gifts 1984), p. 60

Christians who all suffered from spiritual, emotional, and physical trauma and received deliverance from generational curses, strongholds, and trouble.

Joel Wesley Morgan, also known as Wess Morgan, is no stranger to living a broken life. In a YouTube interview on TBN Praise the Lord[200], he shares his testimony, discussing his past and how God changed his life. Wess grew up in a church where his parents were the pastors. Morgan stated that he gave his parents trouble from his early years. At the age of ten, he was drunk for the first time, and at the age of eleven, he smoked pot for the first time. It was at the age of fourteen when he first started smoking crack.

Morgan had trouble in school, including fighting and beating up teachers. He was frustrated and mad at everyone. Morgan was so troubled that his parents eventually lost custody of him, landing him in an alternative school for children. One might conclude that he was experiencing spiritual trauma, resulting in emotional pain that he could not control.

When asked by the interviewer what caused his life to change, he acknowledged the problems in his life. He confessed that he believed there was a spiritual call for his life from which he was running. At this point in his young

---

[200] (W. Morgan 2008), May 18, 2008

life, he had been in and out of jail and prison, and he wanted to get straight to avoid prison time. Morgan committed assault and armed robbery, and he was facing prison time. Morgan confessed that he, in time, got straight. It was the right thing to do, but for the wrong reasons; he wanted to avoid prison time.

Morgan tells viewers that he was able to avoid prison time, and he was released to come home—only to find more trouble. Two and a half years into his marriage, his life went through hell, and he found himself in trouble. He found himself in life-changing trouble whereby he was involved in a bad car accident with two of his friends as passengers. As the friends were airlifted to the hospital, Morgan was hauled off to jail. Something about this visit to jail was different. This time, he prayed. He knew he could avoid the judicial penalties and skate away from trouble. But this time, Morgan wanted God to deliver him from a life of trouble, so he prayed. Morgan says that God answered the prayer and said that if he would come into 100% accountability, his life would change.

Morgan held up his end of the bargain, and so did God. After serving one year in jail, long enough for him to get clean, he was released from prison and sent home with his parents. He said that he did everything to avoid contact with the local drug dealers, including avoiding going to the mailbox where the drug dealers might be and trying to tempt him to do drugs once again. Morgan declared that he did not leave his house without his parents, wife, or someone who would hold him accountable. He knew that he

Wess now sings like a man set free from a life of disaster!

was not strong enough on his own. God used his parents and wife as His agents to watch over Wess until he was strong enough to be healed and delivered.

During the interview, the interviewer proclaimed that Wess now sings like a man set free from a life of disaster! Morgan is known for his songs titled "I Choose to Worship," "You Paid it All," and "Cannot Thank You Enough." God delivered Wess from a life of despair. He understood that his trouble was not only for his benefit but for others. For Morgan, his experience with trouble qualifies him to teach others about Christ. He is now on a crusade to help others through his efforts, not only to recover and hold others accountable but also to prevent. He helps children avoid a life of addiction and trouble even before the enemy can grab them and torment them with curses, strongholds, and trouble.

Eric, whose last name is unknown, although a Christian for twenty years, struggled with pornography and sexual addictions for forty years. Even after becoming a Christian, Eric still struggled. Eric, during a YouTube interview with

Pastor Vladimir Savchuk of Hungry Generation Church, confessed that exposure to an extramarital affair is what led to him being set free from his addictions. Eric proclaimed that the struggles of his heart and his mind caused him to lose everything—his marriage, his family, his job, everything.

Eric acknowledged his need for help, and God began to deal with him to rebuild his life. God met Eric at the lowest point of his life. He met him where he had lost everything and found himself riddled with shame and guilt. God used the exposure of his sin to bring him to repentance, which resulted in redemption. As with Eric, God will sometimes employ exposure, which is painful and shameful, to bring us to a place where we can meet Him. Like Eric, we, too, can slowly begin to rebuild and recover from our sin(s).

Remember the lady, who we called "Redeemed"? She knows all too well what it is like to have so much stolen from her through sin—her sin

> ...generational curse of alcoholism created a life of trouble for "Redeemed" and what became the turning point for her.

and through generational curses of sin. "Redeemed" grew up in Detroit and was the youngest daughter of two siblings. While her parents were both diligent, hardworking people, they experienced their fair share of struggles in life. Both parents came from families who struggled with addiction to alcohol. Because both parents frequently enjoyed alcoholic beverages, there was always alcohol present and accessible in the home. Unfortunately, alcohol was accessible to "Redeemed" as a young child. As a child, she recalls being allowed to have beer on Christmas Eve to celebrate the festivities with the adults. As a teenager, she became one of her father's drinking companions and was allowed to drink in the home regularly. She not only enjoyed drinking an ice-cold beer with Dad, but grew to enjoy more potent alcohol, as well.

This chain of events caused "Redeemed," like many other family members, to become a functioning alcoholic. She went from drinking socially to drinking alone. She enjoyed drinking to the extent that she influenced her loved ones and friends to drink as she did. She became an ambassador for Satan, on a crusade to ruin the lives of others. Alcohol began to ruin her life. Where she once enjoyed drinking, it became a crutch to deal with the misfortunes in her life. More to come on how she was Satan's ambassador. But for now, let us continue to examine how the generational curse of alcoholism created a life of trouble for "Redeemed" and what became the turning point for her.

On December 1, 1991, "Redeemed" dedicated her life to Christ and was baptized as a commitment to her Christian belief. Her grandmother introduced her to Christ as a young child and took her to church, but it was not until her adult years that she developed the desire to have a relationship with God by accepting His son, Jesus, as her Lord. Although she was now in church, attending bible studies, and becoming thirsty for the knowledge of God, her thirst for alcohol was also present. Even after becoming baptized, she was still a functioning alcoholic.

As a functioning alcoholic, she could hold her liquor and not appear drunk in the presence of others. However, there were times when she had too much to drink to the point of becoming drunk and vomiting, hugging the toilet while vomiting and promising never to drink again. Drinking became risky when she would often drink and drive, putting not only her life at risk but others as well. How long could this go on? How long before she gets stopped by the police while drinking and ends up in jail? How long before she kills someone while at the wheel driving drunk? God had plans for her; therefore, something had to change in her life. A turning point was necessary.

It was not until she became pregnant with her first child in 1993, at the age of twenty-eight, that she was able to abstain from drinking. It was then that she realized that she did not want her child to experience the generational curse of alcoholism. By this time in her life, her mother was no longer drinking and had been set free from the grip of alcohol. Praise God!

Although "Redeemed" had stopped using alcohol, the scars from mental, physical, and emotional abuse were ever present, along with guilt, shame, and despair. "Redeemed" struggled with low self-esteem even when she appeared strong and confident in front of others. Not only was depression weighing her down, but anxiety, fear, and doubt were her companions.

By this stage of life, "Redeemed" met college graduates who were successful in their careers. She battled depression because of the time wasted in her life. She was not fulfilled

...she is an ambassador for Christ, on a mission to preach the Good News of salvation...

in life and wondered about her purpose, which brings up another point. Her parents did not stress the importance of getting a college degree. Their main concern was for her to graduate from high school, get a decent job, and take care of herself and her family, which she did. In fact, "Redeemed" not only completed her high school education, but she eventually graduated with her bachelor's and master's degrees years later. She also has a doctorate in Christian Counseling.

Like the testimonies of Wess Morgan and Eric, "Redeemed" began to sense the call of God on her life. She was called into the ministry to teach and preach the Gospel. She is now an ordained pastor, preacher, and clinical mental health counselor. "Redeemed" is on a crusade to help others receive the spiritual healing and deliverance they desire. She was once an ambassador for Satan, teaching others how to sin and live reckless lives. Now, she is an ambassador for Christ, on a mission to preach the Good News of salvation, redemption, and deliverance to those willing to listen to her message.

"Redeemed" understands that sometimes healing and forgiveness happen overnight; other times, it may take months or even years.[201] Furthermore, once achieved, continuous effort is required to maintain healing and deliverance. There will always be something that causes one to experience spiritual, emotional, and physical pain.

I was on my way to hell and spiraling fast. No one knew the pain that I was going through...

A personal relationship intricately connected to God helps deal with life's vicissitudes. Even when dreadful things happen to good people, God is ready to heal and deliver His people, as He has for Wess Morgan, Eric, and "Redeemed."

Let the redeemed of the Lord say so!

People have a great deal in common with biblical characters, Wess, Eric, and "Redeemed" in that they are just

---

[201] (Linn and Linn, *Healing of Memories: Transforming Past Hurts into Gifts* 1984), p. 60

everyday individuals who have experienced traumatic events. We do not have to go far to encounter someone dealing with situations just like ours. They are our neighbors, co-workers, friends, and family. They are people we meet daily. Have you ever met someone in this predicament? If not, meet the lady known as "Redeemed."

Hello, my name is Dr. Lavita Sophia Modest, also known as "Redeemed." I have suffered from spiritual trauma, suffered emotional dysregulation, and physical pain in my life. I, too, have been a victim of generational curses, strongholds of wrong attitudes, wrong patterns of thinking, wrong ideas, and desires. The combination of these forces led to me experiencing trouble in my life. The trouble was self-defeating, self-destructive, and self-damnation. I was on my way to hell and spiraling fast. No one knew the pain that I was going through because my pride would not let me share my story with others. Besides, I was considered one of "the strong friends" in my crowd. How dare I let my circle know that I was indeed suffering. Who could they count on if not me? See what I mean about wrong patterns of thinking?

When I finally realized that I was a sinner who desperately needed a savior, I was tired and weary. Life was beating me down and getting the best of me. I knew I needed someone stronger than me who could help me win in life. From what I had learned about God from my grandmother and other spiritual and influential people, I knew that He was where I could find refuge. Like so many others, God met me during the lowest point in my life when I felt alone and unloved. I prayed to Him to take the taste of alcohol from me and to remove the stains of sin from my life, and He did just that! God saved my life and *redeemed* me from the pit of hell.

After experiencing spiritual, emotional, and physical pain caused by generational trauma/curses and strongholds, I went on a quest to receive spiritual healing and deliverance. There was much work to do as the pain from past trauma had severely and negatively impacted my life. As a result of receiving inner healing and deliverance, I developed *The Modest Model for Healing and Deliverance* to help others achieve the same.

My husband and ministry partner, Chaplain Eric Modest (*different from the "Eric" previously mentioned who previously suffered from pornography addiction*), have been married for thirty-five years. We come from similar family backgrounds. Eric also has family members who also suffer from alcohol dependency. As such, I vowed to break the generational curse of alcoholism in our family and to help others receive healing and deliverance in various areas of life.

Having a solid faith in God and instructing my children the same, as directed by God, is extremely essential to living a lifestyle of spiritual healing and deliverance. Through our faith in God, Eric and I have raised two beautiful children who are both college graduates and who were not plagued by the generational curse of alcoholism! All praises to God! Hallelujah!

EPILOGUE

One of my goals in ministry is to help others receive the spiritual healing and deliverance they desire. Using *The Modest Model for Healing and Deliverance*, others have been blessed to see a positive change in their life. Using the steps identified in *The Modest Model for Healing and Deliverance*, you, too, can achieve spiritual healing and deliverance in your life! It is my prayer that you allow this book to serve as a guide to lead you on a spiritual journey to wholeness. Set aside some dedicated time for self-reflection as you read and reply to the "Points to Ponder" section of this book. Allow the questions to jumpstart your journey to spiritual healing and deliverance.

Remember, GOD is our G.O.D. (giver of deliverance)! He will be with you as you are on your journey to heal from any spiritual or generational trauma that you may be suffering from. You are never alone!

Points to Ponder

1. What does spiritual healing and deliverance mean to you?

_____

_____

_____

_____

2. When have you experienced spiritual trauma that left you with feelings of worthlessness, brokenness, or hopelessness?

_____

_____

_____

_____

3. When digging deep to achieve inner healing, where would you like to begin?

_____

_____

_____

_____

4. Would you like the assistance of others to help you process the trauma, or would prefer to heal under the guidance of the Holy Spirit?

_____

_____

_____

_____

5. What steps have you taken to be more self-aware and conscious of your adverse feelings and emotions?

_____

_____

_____

_____

6. Make a list of past and present trauma and trouble.

_____

_____

_____

_____

7. When do you experience symptoms of anxiety, fear, anger, or guilt the most? Identify any triggers associated with the feelings.

_____

_____

_____

_____

8. What are some negative learned behaviors (family practices/rituals) from childhood that you are currently practicing? These could be related to fear and/or anger.

_____

_____

_____

_____

9. When have you experienced physical, verbal and/or mental abuse? Make a list of those scenarios.

_____

_____

_____

_____

10.What does generational trauma mean to you?

_____

_____

_____

_____

11.Identify family illnesses that may have been passed
down through the bloodline.

_____

_____

_____

_____

12.Do you have a personal relationship with God,
through His son, Jesus Christ?

_____

_____

_____

_____

13. Have you renounced all demonic intrusions that may be at work in your life?

_____

_____

_____

_____

14. Of the seven steps in *The Modest Model for Healing and Deliverance*, which step is the most difficult for you, and why?

_____

_____

_____

_____

15. What rituals or behaviors were practiced in your home growing up that you now recognize as demonic, occult, idol worshipping or even witchcraft?

_____

_____

_____

_____

16.What is your greatest takeaway from reading this
   book?

_____

_____

_____

_____

ABOUT THE AUTHOR

While many counselors and mental health professionals solely seek to help, she seeks to heal. For Dr. Lavita S. Modest, counselor, coach and speakers, spiritual healing, deliverance and wholeness aren't optional. They are must-haves for every believer of Jesus Christ. As a beacon of hope for the hopeless, and a compass for the lost, Dr. Lavita is intentional about leaving people better than they were when she found them—mentally, spiritually, physically and emotionally.

As a licensed counselor, Dr. Lavita holds a Bachelor of Biblical Studies, a Master of Clinical Mental Health Counseling, and a Doctorate of Christian Counseling. In addition to serving as an adjunct professor and University Program Supervisor, Dr. Lavita oversees master level students in their pursuit to become clinical counselors, as well as the fieldwork for new clinicians as they pursue full licensure. Passionate about seeing people healed through the counseling process, whether clinical or spiritual healing, she strategically developed a seven-step process, *The Modest Model for Healing and Deliverance*, a simplistic guide to help individuals begin the process of overcoming past and present trauma.

In her debut book, *The Modest Model for Healing and Deliverance*, Dr. Lavita not only ushers readers into spiritual healing and deliverance—she guides them on an intimate spiritual journey to wholeness and freedom. Complete with moments of self-reflection and "Points to Ponder," this book explores the mind-body connection that promotes spiritual, emotional, and physical healing, and deliverance from generational curses and strongholds many have strived to break for decades. As a non-empirical, theoretical-based study, evidence of healing and deliverance are found using biblical examples and real-life testimonies from everyday people— making this literary masterpiece real, raw and relatable.

As a candid counselor, transformational public speaker and mentor to many, numerous doors of opportunity have opened for Dr. Lavita. In addition to serving as a Public Service Chaplain through the Public Service Institute, she is also a Certified Life Coach through the International Association of Professional Career College. Installed as Senior Pastor of Creation Christian Community, Dr. Lavita is wholeheartedly committed to spearheading a counseling and community ministry, reaching people outside of the four walls of church. As the President and Founder of Creation Christian Counseling, as well as Working Wellness

Solutions, LLC, she provides spiritual, biblical, and clinical mental health counseling for men and women across the Metro-Detroit area.

For booking or speaking engagements, email TMM4SHAD@gmail.com or call 313.335.7435. You can also visit Dr. Lavita on the web at www.drlavitaspeaks.com.

BIBLIOGRAPHY

Allender, PhD., Dan B. 1999. *The Healing Path: How the Hurts in Your Past Can Lead You To A More Abundant Life*. Wheaton, Illinois: Waterbrook.

APA. 2022. *Diagnostic and Statistical Manual of Mental Disorders*, Fifth Edition, Text Revision. Washington, DC: American Psychiatric Association, 2022.

Berding, Kenneth. 2022. Kindle Afresh. August 20. Accessed Novembeer 28, 2023. https://kennethberding.com/2022/08/20/what-is-a-stronghold-2-corinthians-104-5/#:~:text=So%2C%20what%20is%20a%20stronghold,against%20the%20knowledge%20of%20God.

Bonanno, George A. 2021. *The End of Trauma: How the New Science of Resilience is Changing How We Think About PTSD*. New York, New York: Basic Books.

Bradley Hagerty, Barbara. 2009. *Fingerprints of God: The Search for the Science of Spirituality*. New York, New York: Penguin Group.

Dictionary, Cambridge. 2023. Dictionary.cambridge.org. October 12. Accessed October 12, 2023.

https://dictionary.cambridge.org/us/dictionary/engl
ish/spiritual.

Fleagle, Arnold R. 2022. *A Psalm for Every Season: 30 Devotions to Discover, Encouragement, Hope, and Beauty*. Minneapolis, Minnesota: Chosen Books.

Harrigton, Ken, and Jeanne Harrington. 2011. *From Curses to Blessings: Removing Generational Curses*. Shippensburg, Pennsylvania: Destiny Image Publishers, Inc.

Hindson, Ed E. 2002. *Holy Bible King James Version*. Grand Rapids, Michigan: Zondervan.

Hull, Megan. 2022. *Fear vs. Phobia: What's the Difference*. Edited by Megan Hull. May 26. Accessed January 04, 2024.
https://www.therecoveryvillage.com/mental-
health/phobias/fear-vs-phobia/.

Jampolsky, M.D., Gerald G. 1999. *Forgiveness: The Greatest Healer of All*. Hillsboro, Oregon: Beyond Words Publishing, Inc.

Kendra Cherry, , MSEd. 2022. *Very Well MInd*. November 08. Accessed October 14, 2023.
https://www.verywellmind.com/what-is-self-
determination-theory-2795387#:~:text=Self%2Dd
etermined%20people%20have%20an,Have%20hig
h%20self%2Dmotivation.

Kylstra, Chester, and Betsy Kylstra. 2005. *Biblical Healing and Deliverance: A Guide to Experiencing Freedom From Sins of the Past. Destructive Beliefs, Emotional &*

Spiritual Pain. curses and Opression. Bloomington , Minnesotq: Chosen Books.

Linn, Dennis, and Matthew Linn. 1977. *Healing Memories Through the Five Stages of Forgiveness*. New York, New York: Paulist Press.

—. 1984. *Healing of Memories: Transforming Past Hurts into Gifts*. Mahwah, New Jersey: Paulist Press, Inc.

Lucado, Max. 2013. *God Will Use This for Good: Surving the Mess of Life*. Nashville, Tennessee: Thomas Nelson.

—. 2013. *You'll Get Through This: Hope and Help for Your Turbulent Times*. Nashville, Tennessee: Thomas Nelson.

McMinn, Ph.D, Mark R. 2011. *Psychology, Theology, and Spirituality in Christian Counseling*. Carol Stream, Illinois: Tyndale House Publishers, Inc.

Merriam-Webster. 2023. Merriam-webster.com/dictionary. October 12. Accessed October 12, 2023. https://www.merriam-webster.com/dictionary/spiritual.

Moore, Beth. 2009. *Praying God's Word: Breaking Free from Spiritual Strongholds*. Nashville, Tennessee: B&H Publishing Group.

Morgan, Mannette. 2019. *Finding Your Voice: A Path To Recovery for Survivors of Abuse*. Issaqah, Washington: Made For Success Publishing.

Morgan, Wess. 2008. YouTube. May 18. Accessed January 14, 2024.

https://www.youtube.com/watch?v=M5KR6-PLK9k.

Newberg, M.D., Andrew, and Mark R. Waldman. 2009. *How God Changes Your Brain: Breakthrough Findings from a Leading Neuroscientist*. New York, New York: The Random House Publishing Group.

Nori, Don. 2005. *Breaking Generational Curses: Releasing God's Power in Us, Our Children, and Our Destiny*. Shippenburg, Pennsylvania: Destiny Image Publishers, Inc.

Raypole, Crystal. 2020. *Let it Out: Dealing with Repressed Emotions*. March 31. Accessed November 13, 2023. https://www.healthline.com/health/repressed-emotions#releasing-them.

Sandford, John, and Mark Sandford. 1998. *A Comprehensive Guide to Deliverance and Inner Healing*. Grand Rapids, Michigan: Chosen Books.

Sandford, John, and Paula Sandford. 1985. *Healing the Wounded Spirit*. Tulsa, Oklahoma: Victory House, Inc.

Sanford, John L., and R. Loren Sanford. 1991. *The Renewal of the Mind*. Tulsa, Oklahoma: Victory House Publishers.

Savard, Liberty. 1998. *Shattering Your Strongholds: Freedom From Your Struggles*. North Brunswick, New Jersey: Bridge-Logos Publishers.

Savchuk, Vladimir. 2023. Youtube. March 14. Accessed January 14, 2024. https://www.youtube.com/watch?v=lxBvRpou6Vo.

Settecase, Joel. 2022. *Is Sola Scriptura Biblical.* August 20. Accessed January 12, 2024. https://thethink.institute/articles/is-sola-scriptura-biblical.

Tolle, Eckhart. 1999. *The Power of Now: A Guide to Spiritual Enlightenment.* Vancouver, Bristish Columia: Namaste Publishing, Inc.

Vallotton, Kris. 2020. *Spiritual Intelligence: The Art of Thinking Like God.* Bloomington, Minesota: Choosen Books.

Van Der Kolk, M.D., Bessel. 2014. *The Body Keeps Score: Brain, Mind, and Body in the Healing of Trauma.* New York, New York: Penguin Books.

Vanderbush, Bill, and Brit Eaton. 2020. Recklace Grace: *The Gift. The Mystery.* The Embrace. Savage, Minnesota: Broadstreet Publishing Group, LLC.

2023. *What Is the Difference between the Soul and the Spirit?* May 9. Accessed October 14, 2023. https://blog.biblesforamerica.org/difference-between-soul-and-spirit/.

Winston, Bill. 2009. *The Law of Confession: Revolutionze Your Life and Rewrite Your Future with the Power of Words.* Tulsa, Oklahoma: Harrison House Publishers.

Zondervan. 1989. *Holy Bible New Revised Standard Version.* Grand Rapids: Zondervan Publishing.

Zondevan. 2002. *Holy Bible New International Version.* Grand Rapids, Michigan: Zondervan.

* 9 7 9 8 9 9 9 3 6 0 6 0 1 *